FRIENDS & CROCODILES
and
GIDEON'S DAUGHTER

screenplays

Stephen Poliakoff, born in December 1952, was appointed writer in residence at the National Theatre for 1976 and the same year won the *Evening Standard*'s Most Promising Playwright award for *Hitting Town* and *City Sugar*. He has also won a BAFTA award for the Best Single Play for *Caught on a Train* in 1980, the *Evening Standard*'s Best British Film award for *Close My Eyes* in 1992, The Critics' Circle Best Play Award for *Blinded by the Sun* in 1996 and the Prix Italia and the Royal Television Society Best Drama award for *Shooting the Past* in 1999. His plays and films include *Clever Soldiers* (1974), *The Carnation Gang* (1974), *Hitting Town* (1975), *City Sugar* (1975), *Heroes* (1975), *Strawberry Fields* (1977), *Stronger than the Sun* (1977), *Shout Across the River* (1978), *American Days* (1979), *The Summer Party* (1980), *Bloody Kids* (1980), *Caught on a Train* (1980), *Favourite Nights* (1981), *Soft Targets* (1982), *Runners* (1983), *Breaking the Silence* (1984), *Coming in to Land* (1987), *Hidden City* (1988), *She's Been Away* (1989), *Playing with Trains* (1989), *Close My Eyes* (1991), *Sienna Red* (1992), *Century* (1994), *Sweet Panic* (1996), *Blinded by the Sun* (1996), *The Tribe* (1997), *Food of Love* (1998), *Talk of the City* (1998), *Remember This* (1999), *Shooting the Past* (1999), *Perfect Strangers* (2001) for which he won the Dennis Potter Award at the 2002 BAFTAs and Best Writer and Best Drama at the Royal Television Society Awards, and *The Lost Prince* (2003), which won three Emmy Awards in 2005 including Outstanding Mini Series.

FRIENDS & CROCODILES

and

GIDEON'S DAUGHTER

Stephen Poliakoff

Introduced by the author

Methuen

Published by Methuen 2005

1 3 5 7 9 10 8 6 4 2

First published in 2005 by
Methuen Publishing Limited,
11–12 Buckingham Gate,
London SW1E 6LB

Methuen Publishing Limited Reg. No. 3543167

A CIP catalogue record for this book is available from
the British Library

ISBN 0 413 77560 7

Typeset by Country Setting, Kingsdown, Kent
Printed and bound in Great Britain by Bookmarque Ltd,
Croydon, Surrey

Introduction

'Why on earth do you want to write for television?'

I was squashed in the corner of a pub in Shepherds Bush and the person who had put this question to me was barely visible through clouds of seventies cigarette smoke. He was a rather supercilious BBC script editor, languid and opinionated, and as he stared at me, clearly rather pleased with his question, I could see a chubby stripper performing over his left shoulder in an adjoining room in the pub.

The date was the winter of 1974 and my twenty-second birthday was the following day. I remember the question with intense clarity and I can recall the interior of the pub in almost supernatural detail but I have absolutely no memory of what sort of answer I gave him; not a single phrase has stayed with me.

Over the intervening three decades that particular question has recurred many times, put to me by all sorts of people, and it has become increasingly difficult to answer.

Back in the early seventies I knew exactly what I *felt* about television drama, I did not have to think for a second, whatever answer I managed to splutter out to that glacial script editor. I believed passionately that television was where you found the most exciting and the best drama. It was where thrilling plays spilled out at you in a constant intoxicating stream. There were nearly always four or five new plays on each week across the BBC and ITV, and though many did not work of course there seemed to be at least one extraordinary new piece every month.

While the British film industry had collapsed and a home-grown cinema movie was as rare a sight as a whale swimming up the Thames, the television in my little flat in west London was blazing out vivid visions of life in Britain straight at me week after week.

The theatre was the place where I was then working exclusively and where I spent most of my nights when there was no play to see on television (for these were the days before video recorders, when you had to stay in if you wanted to see something). I had already had two or three stage plays on professionally and I was soon to have the eerie experience of having five of my plays performed in London in the same calendar year, causing descriptions of me in the press to travel from the ominous 'a promising writer' to the more deadly 'a veteran playwright'. I adored being part of the theatre (and still do) and I saw every new play that was on in London, but I often found myself sitting almost alone in the auditorium. It is easy to rewrite the past or to misremember it, and because the seventies was a particularly rich time for new writing in the theatre it is possible to forget that very few of the British theatre-going public wanted to go and see these plays.

I vividly remember watching a new play in the main auditorium at the Royal Court one evening, surrounded by just seven other people. Several remarkable new plays of the period played to tiny houses, despite generating a great deal of attention from the press. I was to experience some of this audience indifference first-hand when my early plays were staged at the Bush Theatre. Though two of the three works I had on there were packed out (the theatre seated only a hundred people), I found it an almost impossible task to get any of my twenty-something friends to go and see my plays – even when I offered to buy them a meal afterwards. These were plays that were considered hits and still they would not go. The reason they gave was that the theatre was for old people or for members of the acting profession to go and admire each other, but what they wanted to see was *Mean Streets* again or *Badlands* or *The Godfather II* (because it was an incredible period for American cinema) and they also wanted to watch television plays. They needed no persuasion to crowd around the television in the evening and watch almost any new drama.

Television was sexy, sometimes literally so because as censorship had thawed dramatically seventies television was liberally scattered with vigorous bouts of copulation, whether it was in a dramatised documentary about Modigliani or a drama series about the exploits of a backbench Labour MP. However there was another altogether far more compelling reason for watching television drama, which was that as an audience you never knew what to expect, you had absolutely no clue what surprising vision was going to come at you across the carpet. It could be as strange and perverse as the hallucinatory journey of an encyclopaedia salesman wandering across the Yorkshire Moors, as mainstream as a group of gangsters ruling over seventies Birmingham, as poetic as two schoolgirls carrying a giant cheese through the outskirts of a northern town, or as surreal as John Gielgud trying to seduce a young Felicity Kendall in a play set in a London embassy.

The public that would not venture into the theatre to see the new work of all these dramatists would tune in readily in great numbers to watch these plays in their living rooms. Now of course one of the reasons for this was there was no escape for the audience from the single play. The viewers often faced a night when on the three channels two of them were showing plays scheduled against each other, so whatever happened a large proportion of the audience were going to have to watch them. These were homes without computers, without the internet and with no DVD players; there was simply nothing else to do. Yet this is only a partial explanation of why these plays did so well. The main reason why viewers were drawn to them was because these were works that either reflected a contemporary Britain back to them, or took them on imaginative journeys which they had not gone on before to destinations they did not expect or did not know existed.

The 'Wednesday Play' and the 'Play for Today' strand that succeeded it (and the many ITV single-play strands which are too often forgotten) are often caricatured as being exclusively fly-on-the-wall social-realist dramas set in prisons, school playgrounds and windswept housing estates; leftwing works made by members of revolutionary splinter groups who were so out of touch with the audience that they totally failed to predict the rise of Margaret Thatcher. Leaving aside the fact that this is a gross distortion of what these social-realist plays were really like, it is fair to point out that they made up only a tiny proportion of the output, because this flood of single plays covered the whole gamut of the human imagination from science fiction, to the political dream plays of David Mercer, to the works of Dennis Potter.

So was this the fabled Golden Age of television drama?

There is a paradox here. All this activity in drama, the countless original plays and drama series were presided over by television mandarins who were not particularly sophisticated and in some cases were the most philistine people I have ever met in show business. The heads of channels were often drawn from Light Entertainment or Sport and would make remarks to you such as, 'You drama people think you're terribly clever, but covering the tennis at Wimbledon is far more difficult than anything you do – because one never knows where the ball is going to go!'

They were simply from another planet and had no vocabulary and no interest in discussing your work. These men, because the ruling class in television was totally male in those days, thought that the original work that crowded the schedules on their channels had no lasting value, no cultural significance of any kind. Hence the number of plays made on videotape from this period that were merrily wiped and have therefore vanished forever. Television was ephemeral and infinitely disposable, and in the view of these men was best forgotten the morning afterwards. In fact they positively disliked the idea of a work lurking around in people's imagination and memory too long, or being given too much fanfare or praise by the press, in case the creators of the work became presumptuous and started demanding more money.

If this was a Golden Age there was certainly no appreciation or encouragement for the work from the top. What is more, below the broadcasting ruling class the atmosphere in which all this drama was made was surprisingly venomous and hostile. The mood of the film and studio crews that made my early plays at the BBC was dark, depressed and deeply unpleasant. Because the technicians in ITV were paid so much more money for doing precisely the same job there was always, in my experience, a mutinous tension hanging around the production of any show at the BBC during this time. There were endless industrial disputes: some blew over in a few days, others festered on for month after month causing the cancellation of many shows. The industrial strife that was being played out all over Britain was particularly acute in the broadcasting industry.

The crews were not just hostile to their paymasters but sometimes to the material they were working on as well. I overheard one technician protesting vigorously during the filming of my train drama, *Caught on a Train*, that starred Peggy Ashcroft and Michael Kitchen, 'There's no sex in this, no violence, I don't know why we're making this shit!' He turned to address the set, a crowded railway carriage, not noticing that I was standing right behind him: 'Can anybody tell me why on earth we're making this?!'

I then piped up, making a stilted defence of my vision in front of an astonished crew before diving out of the (stationary) railway carriage into the night. I was seething with self-doubt and began yelling out as I wandered on the platform, 'How could I have been so stupid . . . ?! Why oh why didn't I have some sex and violence . . . ?!'

So I can promise you it did not feel like a Golden Age at the time.

By contrast the crews I film with now as I direct my dramas are full of enthusiasm and a desire to make something special, a sentiment I never heard expressed during the seventies and eighties.

Even the buildings themselves from which all this stimulating production was at that time pouring seemed to exude the same sense of bitterness and neglect as the employees. Television Centre, though a relatively new building when I first ventured into it in 1974, appeared to be a place that had never been young, never been excited about anything. Its circular corridors filled the spirit with an immediate sense of dread and paranoia (and still do). Lime Grove, where I used to go to watch cuts of my films being projected in a funny little prefab screening room, had a tangle of endless rotting corridors and spooky almost comically shabby studios. This is where Hitchcock had made *The Thirty Nine Steps* and yet there was no pleasurable sense of the ghosts of British cinema haunting the passages, just a feeling of squalor.

The atmosphere in the ITV companies was a little better because people were richer, but there was the same sense of potential industrial conflict lurking on each filming day, of barely disguised rage hovering near the surface, and no shoot was complete without one or two grim confrontations.

Yet mingling all the time with this dispiriting atmosphere of perpetual industrial unrest was the artistic anarchy, the creative partnership of writers, producers and directors who, given almost total freedom, were constantly experimenting and setting themselves new challenges. Each drama producer had their own slot of five or six plays a year and they commissioned these works themselves, so the schedules were full of a host of different tastes. There was no central control through which every work had to pass; no channel controller ever read any of my scripts during these years. He would have been extremely shocked to have been asked to do so.

This diversity in the plays department was stimulating and made for a highly competitive atmosphere, although the creative community was naturally no happier than the technicians: we were always moaning, always feeling underappreciated. There were constant complaints that there were not enough slots for plays. In reality it is truly startling to look up the schedules of that period and realise just how much drama there actually was. It was a time when nobody had ever heard of focus groups and there were no committees fuelled by half-digested American business plans trying to tell drama practitioners how to make better plays. There were instead just the wild imaginings of a whole generation of writers. Of course at the time none of us appreciated how precious this creative anarchy was or how short-lived it would turn out to be. Sometime, maybe in the late eighties, it was extinguished forever.

How good were these works? Did this stream of plays yield up any significant number of pieces that would stand the test of time?

It is an intriguing and complex question. Obviously there are a handful of iconic works of the sixties and seventies (and a few from the eighties) that people would immediately cite: *Cathy Come Home, Blue Remembered Hills, Tinker Tailor Soldier Spy* etc. There are occasional chances to see a tiny percentage of the work from this period on BBC4 if you are very alert and study your TV listing guide closely.

However, the vast bulk of the drama of the sixties and seventies is lost, not technically because all the work made on film still exists, but lost in the sense of living on only in the ledgers of a few television archivists.

In any other art form one would naturally turn to the work of critics and academics to find out what was of value from the past. Unfortunately the level of most academic writing on television drama has consistently proved to be extremely thin and unimpressive. I personally do not know of a single good book on British television drama and if there is one it has remained curiously hidden. The lack of good scholarship on this subject is a quite extraordinary state of affairs, because a strong case could be made for television drama being the most significant art form of the late twentieth century in Britain.

In the various archives across the country there exist well over two thousand full-length television plays which nobody has evaluated or seen since they originally went out. Many of these are by famous writers or star some of our greatest actors. Slowly a few of these works are surfacing from this black hole but there is very little information available for a new generation to know where to begin, what to ask for, what to try to reclaim.

Most writing on broadcasting either concentrates on tracing the history, the power shifts especially within the BBC, or else buys into the theory which first came to prominence in the eighties that the most worthwhile drama on television is to be found in soap operas and police series. This is a school of thinking that oddly links straight back to the philistine monsters of seventies broadcasting – television is only good if it is aiming both to be popular and ephemeral. Television as art is a dirty word, only used by pretentious theatre writers who have wandered into television by accident. Of course there *is* great soap opera from time to time, and most cultural observers would now accept that; what absolutely nobody seems to accept however is that lying somewhere in the maze of television archives are works of enduring beauty, true works of art which have totally disappeared off the critical radar.

If I am right and there is no detailed academic research on the single play to draw on – despite the forest of media courses in our universities – and there are no reliable critics that are experts on this period, then one is left without a guide to lead us through all this vanished work, just the memory of the audience and the memory of the practitioners and the dramatists. Therefore I cannot really address the question 'How good were these plays?', and nor at the moment can anyone else. Clearly *some* of them were good because they have stayed in my memory for over thirty years. These works have fed my imagination more than anything else and their influence on me is still being felt and is indeed reflected in the screenplays in this volume. What we may never know, unless some talented person dedicates their life to it, is how *much* of this work was of lasting value.

However, there is one thing that is very clear about that time, although there was intense artistic snobbery about television (indeed *The Times* did not even have a TV critic all through the seventies) nobody could say then, 'I never watch television, there's nothing but rubbish on it,' and expect to be taken seriously.

Yet today it is hardly possible to open any newspaper

without coming across some supposedly important personage boasting exactly that. Recently I read a cultural commentator trumpeting, 'Nobody I know has watched television for at least five years!' In the *Guardian* 'My Media' column, figures prominent in some way in the zeitgeist are constantly popping up saying the only TV they ever watch 'is *The Sopranos* and *Newsnight*'. It has become one of the most lamentable and predictable clichés of recent years. Obviously these people must think coming out with such a statement in print makes them seem sexier, more original, so busy being creative and interesting they cannot watch television. Personally if I read somebody saying that, I know immediately I am not going to be interested in anything else they have to say. However, clearly they feel at the moment they can get away with it.

So is current television so bad?

There is certainly no mood of anarchy, no sprouting of a hundred different voices as there was in my youth. There are of course many great shows still, brilliant comedy, and the authored drama – the dramatist's personal vision – is making a tentative comeback.

Yet there is no denying in television drama especially there has been a great aching loss.

Many of the senior writers of the country, those now in their sixties and seventies, turned their back on television about twenty years ago and have scarcely been back since. They have preferred to supplement their income from the theatre by writing screenplays for Hollywood. The financial rewards for doing this are obviously high but the artistic satisfaction can be severely limited because, as is always the case with the film industry, very few of these screenplays ever get made. What is more, in the rare instance they do get into production they have often been rewritten by a whole clutch of other writers. This is one of the reasons I have personally always steered clear of Hollywood despite several interesting encounters with directors and producers over the years. Throughout my career I have found the idea of being told how to write fairly nightmarish. For better or worse, I have wanted my voice to end up on the screen undiluted.

A lot of other writers, both of my generation and the one before, fell out of favour with television executives during the last two decades and could not get their work on the screen despite still being passionately keen to write for television. No doubt there is a mixture of circumstances to explain why this happened, but there is undoubtedly one reason that links each case – the executives in question had become suspicious and fearful of originality, of anything mysterious, of the unexpected.

I would probably have found myself in the same predicament as these writers if it had not been for two lucky circumstances. The first was my decision about eighteen years ago to start directing all my own work. The consequence of this was that, just as power began to centralise in all broadcasting outlets, executives found when they were dealing with me they were arguing with and being challenged by one unified voice. A voice that could not for instance be easily fobbed off with the perennial excuse, 'We're still looking for the right director for your piece . . .'

The second reason for my survival was that the least expensive piece of television I ever wrote, *Shooting the Past*, my trilogy about a photographic library fighting to stay alive, had a far bigger impact than anybody had anticipated. Despite the fact that it cost so little, there were many people at the BBC who were very nervous about it; it was scheduled late at night and even the continuity announcer's voice shook with uncertainty when she introduced it.

Its success startled everybody, including me. It happened to be first transmitted when a lot of authored drama had disappeared from the screen and the audience seemed to respond to it as if they had been suffering from a great thirst.

I fought very hard behind the scenes to keep *Shooting the Past* in the form that I had written and directed it. There had been a concerted effort by various executives after I had finished it to make me quicken its pace, to slash thirty-five minutes out of it, to change its form out of all recognition. I responded to all this interference with undisguised fury, announcing the piece would not change even if it meant I never wrote for television again.

Because the audience responded to *Shooting the Past* nobody has tried to interfere with any of my subsequent work and I have achieved artistic freedom.

If that was taken away from me I would immediately stop writing for television.

I would be lying if I said I was absolutely confident from the outset that *Shooting the Past*, paced so slowly by the standards of the time, would hold its audience. The fact that it did supported my instinct that the audience had not really changed from when I was young. There may be hundreds of channels, there may be a whole new technology, but the viewers still have catholic tastes, they want drama paced in all sorts of ways, they want surprises. They are drawn both to dramas that are hallucinatory and dreamlike and those that are loud, fast and rasping.

The idea that all drama should become a homogenised slick stream is the quickest way to ratings ruin for any broadcaster.

Therefore it was a conjunction of circumstances that allowed me to continue writing in the same way for television as I had always done. Put simply, it meant writing what interested me and hoping it would interest the audience too.

I am glad to say in the last few years, almost simultaneously with my continuing journey in television, a group of other writers (admittedly a small group) has experienced creative freedom too. The works of Russell T. Davis, Paul Abbott, Abi Morgan, Jimmy McGovern and Tony Marchant, amongst others, have kept the authored television drama very much alive. The success of this work shows that the writer's vision on television can still have an impact on the national consciousness despite the multi-channel reality-TV times we live in.

What is more, we dramatists have seen our work have the further life that an earlier generation of writers was denied – DVD has finally stopped television being ephemeral. Now, at last, it is emphatically an enduring art form, although its future status clearly depends on enough talented people being given the freedom to create it.

It would be disingenuous of me not to own up to the fact that my position as a writer-director with creative freedom is of course a highly privileged one and that I may be a member of a dying breed.

Nowadays the media buildings that young writers walk into at the start of their careers are no longer rotting and squalid and full of venomous industrial unrest, but are gleaming and full of light, seemingly bursting with aspiration and optimism. However, behind the clean white surfaces there lurks an oppressive central control, a worship of the predictable, and an almost universal reluctance amongst those working in television to challenge their bosses for fear of losing their job.

There is a new paradox in broadcasting: those currently running it are nearly all much brighter and more cultured than the executives I remember from my youth, but the programmes they are presiding over are often much dumber than those their predecessors gave us. The broadcasting bosses of today argue that they are facing a much more competitive market than the one that existed in the last century. This is true up to a point (the battle between ITV and BBC1 was often ferocious in the past), but these executives are guilty none the less of greatly underestimating their audience. The present broadcasting elite spends millions every year on battalions of outside experts, committees and focus groups, trying to second-guess the future in an attempt to control the uncontrollable and beat the uncertainty created by each new wave of technology. They forget that nearly all successes come from an individual or a small group of people passionately committed to an idea. Almost all hits originate from unexpected quarters, or from familiar quarters having unexpected ideas, and often these creative people are difficult, will not fit neatly into any business plan, and are impossible to categorise. Moreover these practitioners will come up with ideas that are not immediately comparable to anything that has gone before; they will not be pale imitations of last year's hits or variations of what other channels have got. The media bosses, when confronted by these ideas, will have no yardstick to measure them against. At the current time, the executive's natural instinct is to reject all such ideas or leave them perpetually floundering on the backburner.

If seventies anarchy was to reign once more there would undoubtedly be more hits on television because any correct reading of broadcasting history powerfully suggests that giving talent its head is the least risky course, the safest way to television glory for the fearful executive.

However, this is a lesson that swims so defiantly against the tenor of the times it has no hope of being implemented. When our government is more centralised than it has ever been, it is hardly likely that broadcasters will merrily give gifted people creative freedom. Moreover, there is a fiction that took hold in the Birt era that somehow giving the individual too much scope for self-expression leads to indulgence and disaster. Of course there are a few examples of that through the broadcasting ages, but then again there are absolutely *no* examples of great shows created by committees.

Nevertheless, despite all the obstacles, there *are* opportunities for the new writer at the present time. If talent refuses to give up, but holds on to its audacity and self-belief, it can chip away at all this centralised control for the simple reason there is just so much airtime to fill at the moment. As the multitude of digital channels proliferate, the need for more and more programmes will make it impossible to keep new talent down for long – somewhere it will find an outlet and burst through.

So there is some hope. What is not so clear at the moment is whether the spirit of the single play, all those different voices that emerged out of awkward people in smoke-filled offices, will ever be seen again in any form.

One might ask, what on earth is the spirit of the single play?

I would answer: a story that does not have to be in a genre, that is definitely not being forced into the shape of a thriller, a soap opera, a medical drama, or a supernatural mystery; a story that just creates its own world, a place you may never have seen before. That is what I witnessed night after night in my youth and these are the images and stories that have stayed with me for a lifetime.

Friends & Crocodiles and *Gideon's Daughter* are works that attempt to carry the spirit of the single play into our present broadcasting climate. They are firstly both single, separate stories though linked by one character, Sneath, played by Robert Lindsay. I found I needed this character to help me write the stories, for I saw him as a slightly parasitical minor-league man of letters, a gossip and hack writer, who none the less knew some things we did not – the stories behind the surface of the times.

Taken together, the films, I hope, complement each other – one being quite an epic story, one very intimate – as they attempt to define some feelings about the present, about now, and how we have ended up where we are. But the two stories do this by looking at the recent past.

In *Friends & Crocodiles* I have tried to write about the recent past in a way that is unexpected. The difficulty about setting a story in times that we all remember is we know what happened – we know Margaret Thatcher reigned for a long time and then fell and eventually there was Tony Blair. In telling the story of Paul and Lizzie I wanted to put us in a position where we do not know what is going to happen. Here is a relationship that is governed by work – a work marriage. Work dominates all our lives and yet is something that is very difficult to write about for the screen. The market place is impatient of anything about work, it can tolerate it being there at the start of a movie but then there is an imperative for the story to turn into a romantic comedy.

I have always wanted to write a relationship between a man and a woman which was not a conventional love story. Relationships at work are frequently as obsessive as any sexual relationship, because one so often wants to be respected by the person one is working for. But that person can disappoint us, or take us for granted, or be wilful and undisciplined and squander the real chance of us achieving something together. Sometimes we find ourselves working with people who we admire greatly but who are just so infuriatingly different from ourselves that eventually the working relationship is destroyed.

Afterwards we are haunted for years about what might have been.

In *Friends & Crocodiles* I have tried to create a story that both dramatises this sort of relationship and also simultaneously throws up memories and responses amongst the audience about the last twenty years and how things have changed.

It begins in the early eighties when the last moments of seventies anarchy were still reverberating through the country, and moves through the world of centralised control and mission statements and absolute belief in a simplified vision of the future, to the near present where it ends on a note of elegiac regret and questioning.

The story separates into four islands: the major opening section set around Paul's great house; the venture capitalists' section; the dark café and the wedding scene, where we see Paul at his lowest ebb; and the last section, where we watch the powerful firm Lizzie is working for disintegrate.

It is in many ways the most ambitious story I have ever tried to tell in its combination of public sweep and its unconventional love story.

The action of *Gideon's Daughter* is set over only a few months, in contrast to the timescale of *Friends & Crocodiles*. The months in question are the summer of 1997, the days and weeks that followed Labour's first election victory after eighteen years of Tory rule, a summer of great expectation that was punctuated in the most dramatic fashion by the death of Princess Diana. Suddenly the country and our television screens were awash with flowers and an outpouring of public grief the like of which very few people could remember in their lifetime.

Against this background I wanted to write a story about private grief and about alienation from the present. In Gideon's personal journey, I wanted to show a man who understands clearly the limitations of his job as a public relations guru and is increasingly alarmed and isolated by the seriousness with which the outside world treats everything he says and does.

Instead of showing the world of public relations as a place of hustlers and liars, I wanted the audience to become Gideon, to enter his head, to see the modern world through his eyes. The PR man is in fact the purest character on show, the one most honestly trying to get to grips with his fears and the contradictions of the times.

Our fears for our children in this increasingly dangerous world run through nearly every parent's mind every day of their lives as they try to get on with their work. If this fear mingles with guilt about how one has behaved as the children were growing up, it can make for an extremely powerful cocktail of feelings that gnaws into one's self-belief and sense of self-worth. This is what happens to Gideon.

I wanted to show a character arriving in this position while doing a very public job, constantly meeting and interacting with the powerful and the famous.

As Gideon's confidence slips away he collides with a very different sort of character, Stella, somebody who has lost her child but who is battling her grief with bravery and eccentric energy. She has no interest in celebrity, no obsession with what is fashionable. She seems to be the only person who might be able to prevent Gideon descending into his darkness.

Through their love story I have tried to dramatise the sense of emptiness a lot of us feel about our rulers and, at the same time, to celebrate the imaginative power of 'normal people'. These are the very same people who will be watching the film on television and into whose homes I will be lucky enough to be able to pour my vision of things. Over a period of time following transmission I will then get to hear by a variety of means – the internet, letters, chance encoun-

ters – how some of them reacted to these two stories. Whatever happens to the shows in the ratings war, I will reach a
large number of people. My picture of the recent past will
have collided with their imaginations and their memories.

That is a great privilege and that is the fundamental
reason why I am still drawn to write for television.

Stephen Poliakoff
October 2005

FRIENDS AND CROCODILES

Friends & Crocodiles was produced by Talkback Productions Ltd for BBC Television and was first screened in January 2006 by BBC1. The cast was as follows:

Paul	Damian Lewis
Lizzie	Jodhi May
Sneath	Robert Lindsay
Anders	Patrick Malahide
Butterworth	Eddie Marsan
Marcus	Allan Corduner
Redfern	Chris Larkin
Coyle	John Warnaby
The Albert Brothers	Paul Hickey, Tim Plester
Angela	Isabel Brook
Christine	Sophie Hunter
Young Rachel	Sasha Hardway
Older Rachel	Shannon Murray
Young Oliver	Harry Melling
Older Oliver	Ed Tolputt
Graham	Giles Taylor
Carol	Olivia Poulet
Mr Zack	Rod Arthur
Simone	Ruth Miller
Ralph	Philip Battley
Diana	Karen Staples
Young Male Consultant	Jake Broder
Young Red-Haired Man	Murray McArthur
Young Blond-Haired Man	Will Thorp
Dark Bearded Man	Stewart C. Scudamore
Very Tall Thin Man	Robert Wilfort
Virtual-Reality Man	Steven O'Neill
Eleven-Year-Old Boy	Sam Friend

Director Stephen Poliakoff
Producer Nicolas Brown
Line Producer Helen Flint
Music Adrian Johnston
Director of Photography Barry Ackroyd BSC
Editor Clare Douglas
Production Designer James Merifield

A date appears on black:

LONDON 1997

Opening credit sequence.

INT. DAY
We are close on a mirror; it fills the whole screen. In the mirror is the face of SNEATH, *a man of indeterminate age. At this stage of the action he may be in his late forties or early fifties, but it is hard to be completely sure. He has a prosperous, successful air, a little self-satisfied, with a glint of mischief.*

As he is examining his features in the mirror, there is a loud rattling sound on the sound track. We realise we are in a lift descending floor by floor, a heavy old lift with metal gates, as found in London mansion flats, creaking and groaning its way down the building. We stay on the mirror as the lift reaches the ground floor with a sudden thud, jerking SNEATH *out of his reverie, the pleasure of perusing his own image.*

INT. PASSAGES AND LOBBY. DAY
Credit sequence continues.

We cut to a gloomy passage leading from the lift towards the lobby of the huge old mansion block. SNEATH *is ambling towards us, acknowledging the cleaning ladies as he passes. His whole manner is carefree, unhurried. As his bulky frame reaches close to the camera, he suddenly stops. His expression totally changes. He looks surprised, even fearful.*

We cut to what he is looking at. Through the glass doors of the main entrance of the flats can be glimpsed a tall man with very long hair. Rain is falling heavily, but the man is oblivious, moving around in the rain allowing himself to get soaked, watching the entrance. He is staring into the lobby, sometimes his face pressed up to the glass. His whole manner is unsettling; he is a wild-looking figure.

SNEATH *immediately retreats away from the entrance into the shadows. He then scuttles up the staircase to the first landing. From this viewpoint he stares down at the man in the rain, trying to work out if the figure has seen him.*

SNEATH *takes out his mobile phone and dials hastily. The credit sequence finishes.*

INT. MODERN OFFICE. DAY
We cut to an expansive modern office, glass walls; we can see the rest of the open-plan office in the back of shot. The lights are just coming on, the rain bucketing down outside. The atmosphere is chilly and austere. LIZZIE *is sitting behind a large desk, a handsome woman. At this stage of the action she seems in her late thirties. She is sitting very straight, in a rather formal manner. She is dressed expensively, but the colours are muted.*

She answers the phone and we inter-cut between SNEATH *on the landing in the mansion flats and* LIZZIE *in the office.*

SNEATH (*his tone urgent*): Lizzie . . . is it you? Hi! Hope you are well . . . Can't chat I'm afraid . . . Just rung to say Paul is here! Right now . . . (*Then with added emphasis.*) PAUL IS HERE!

LIZZIE: Paul?! . . . Paul is with you?

SNEATH: Not actually with me, no . . . (SNEATH *is staring down at the figure in the rain.*) He is waiting outside the door for me . . . He looks extraordinary too – his hair's really long . . . He looks like he has been living in a cave –

LIZZIE: I haven't been in touch with Paul . . . not for years.

SNEATH: Haven't you? You sure?! I was hoping you might have at least spoken to him.

LIZZIE (*getting more tense*): We haven't spoken, no . . . you
     know that!
SNEATH: You've no idea what he wants, then? You don't
     know why he might want to see me . . . ?
LIZZIE (*hesitates for a second*): No. Not a clue. (*We stay on
     LIZZIE's eyes for a moment.*)

INT. LOBBY. DAY
We cut to SNEATH *approaching across the lobby towards the
glass doors, keeping to the edge of the carpet, in the shadows.*

SNEATH (*whispering to himself*): If I look straight ahead I can
     make it . . .
     *We cut to his POV of his taxi waiting for him by the curb,
     the rain pouring down, and* PAUL *criss-crossing the entrance,
     a dark unruly shape between* SNEATH *and his taxi.*
          SNEATH *steels himself.*

EXT. THE PAVEMENT OUTSIDE MANSION BLOCK. DAY
We cut to SNEATH *emerging from the flats. He has put up a
large umbrella and is making straight for the cab, looking
directly in front of him, determined not to clock anything or
anyone. He seems to have made it, getting the cab door open
and pulling down the umbrella in one scrambled movement,
when a hand falls on his shoulder.*

   SNEATH *turns,* PAUL *is staring down at him through the rain.*

SNEATH (*acts in astonishment*): Paul, is it you? . . . It is
     you . . . ?! How extraordinary – after all this time!
     PAUL *seems totally unfazed by* SNEATH's *performance.*
     He stares calmly through the rain.
PAUL: It is me, yes. How goes it?
SNEATH: It goes well. I think. Very well! And with you . . . ?

You look . . . (*His voice falls away.*)

PAUL *grins, unembarrassed.*

PAUL: Like shit.

SNEATH: No, no, no of course not! I was going to say . . . different certainly! A tiny bit different . . .

He looks at PAUL*'s clothes, which are dark and strange. He then stares straight at* PAUL. *There is something piercing about* PAUL*'s eyes, very watchful, intelligent, no sign of bitterness, but a little frightening nonetheless.*

SNEATH *smiles hastily.*

SNEATH: I mean new hairdo and everything . . . it's quite a change!

PAUL: Busy, are you?

SNEATH: Of course! As always! Busy stirring away, at this and that –

PAUL: Writing your memoirs yet? Publishing a diary? . . . Ready to spill the beans . . .

SNEATH looks truly startled at this insight. He laughs rather too heartily.

SNEATH: How on earth did you know that?! No, only joking – of course I'm not! Definitely not! That won't be for a long while . . .

PAUL *watching him intently.*

PAUL: The stories you could tell . . .

SNEATH: Couldn't I just! (*He laughs.*) I must remember that . . . ! (SNEATH *is desperate to get away.*) You weren't looking for *me*, were you Paul . . . ?

PAUL: Of course.

SNEATH: And why were you doing that . . . ?

PAUL*'s manner is very calm, almost gentle.*

PAUL: Many reasons . . . I think it is time you paid me a visit.

SNEATH *looks very alarmed at this.*

PAUL: You haven't seen where I am living now, have you?

SNEATH: No, that would be good . . . Great! . . . I can't wait to see that . . .

SNEATH *wriggles into the taxi and through the door finishes the conversation.*

SNEATH: Look, Paul, I am terribly late, I have to go to a meeting, it is something rather important, and the meter's running as you can see . . . I am very uncharacteristically paying for this taxi myself . . . So I will phone you tomorrow . . . same number is it? Your mobile . . . ?

PAUL: Never changes.

SNEATH: I will call tomorrow . . . (SNEATH *is mightily relieved to get away from* PAUL; *he starts putting up the window.*) without fail . . . ! (SNEATH *turns to the taxi driver.*) – Go, go, go! Go now! To the Savoy. (*As the driver is slow to respond.*) What you waiting for . . . ? GO! *As the taxi moves off,* SNEATH *looks back through the window. A receding image of* PAUL. *The rain has intensified even more, and through the glass* PAUL'*s dark figure is distorted by the rain drops, as he watches* SNEATH *drive away.*

We watch the figure in the rain disappearing from us and dissolve.

EXT. THE GROUNDS OF THE BIG HOUSE. AFTERNOON
We dissolve from the grey light and the rain to blue water filling the screen. A girl in a bikini is swimming lazily in the pool, the sun glinting on the water.

A title comes up '1981' as the girl criss-crosses the swimming pool.

We see SNEATH *looking nearly twenty years younger, his fresh pink cheeks, his skin gleaming in the heat. His beady eyes are observing everything, with the same glint as in the opening sequence, but he looks a lot less prosperous. He is sitting near the pool eating a large piece of cheesecake.*

All around the pool are young women, most of them ravishing,

*like extras from a Bond film, some in bathing suits soaking in
the sun, others sitting in the shade sipping wine. There is a
sprinkling of men of different ages amongst them: some are in
their twenties, but others are much older. There are a couple of
very senile-looking aristocrats, and some eccentrically-shaped
middle-aged men, ranging from the elegant to the seedy. In all a
collection of faces which is difficult to categorise, the old and the
young are mingled together.*

*Flunkies are waiting on them, spread discreetly round the
pool, keeping to the shadows. The atmosphere is luxurious and
indulgent.*

SNEATH *is sitting next to a very earnest-looking young man,*
REDFERN, *who is absorbed in a huge reference book, making
notes feverishly as he reads.*

REDFERN: Marvellous . . . absolutely marvellous! (*He looks
up and beams at no one in particular.*) There are facts in
here that will make your hair stand on end . . . !
SNEATH *eats his cheesecake, a look of blissful contentment
on his face. He brushes the crumbs off his lips, and as he
does so he glances out of the corner of his eye at some of
the beautiful young women. He then glances across at a
dishevelled-looking man with a ruffled academic
demeanour and wildly old-fashioned clothes. This is*
BUTTERWORTH, *who is eating boiled sweets out of a
paper bag and holding forth to one of the young women
near him.* SNEATH *notices a half-sucked sweet has
somehow got itself stuck to* BUTTERWORTH's *trouser leg.*

*And then we see that, slightly apart from everyone else,
sitting in a fine wicker chair, is* PAUL. *He looks elegant,
poised, beautifully dressed. It is obvious from his
demeanour that he is presiding over the whole gathering.
He is doodling a sketch in a notebook, drawing the heads
of his guests, a cigarette in the corner of his mouth.*

SNEATH *glances across the lawn that slopes down away*

*from the house to a public right of way that crosses the
grounds. A small figure, initially just a tiny dot in the
distance, is walking along the path. She neither stares to
her left or right, as if she is purposely ignoring the pool
and all the guests.*

SNEATH: There she is . . . She is always on time . . . regular
as clockwork.

REDFERN *glances up from his book for a second to stare at
the tiny figure moving along the path, then looks straight
back at his book.*

SNEATH (*mutters to himself*): Nobody seems to have noticed
her except me . . .

SNEATH *watches fascinated as the young figure crosses the
estate. He can glimpse her through gaps in the hedge. We
can now make out it is* LIZZIE.

Suddenly SNEATH *looks back at* PAUL *and sees that*
PAUL's *chair is empty.* SNEATH *glances back at* LIZZIE *as
she continues her progress. He sees that* PAUL *is waiting for
her, at a bend in the path.* PAUL *is one side of the hedge,
and* LIZZIE *is on the other.*

EXT. THE PATH. DAY

We are with LIZZIE *walking along the path. She is in the
foreground, behind her over the hedge is the great house: our
first full view of the house in wide shot in all its magnificence,
and the grounds, which are peppered by little temporary follies,
silver tents, little brightly coloured marquees. We are then even
tighter on* LIZZIE, *she is only looking straight ahead.* PAUL's
voice calls, 'Hi'. LIZZIE *stops.* PAUL *is moving along on the
other side of the hedge. For a moment she can't see him clearly
and then his face appears.* PAUL *repeats his 'Hi'.*

LIZZIE (*politely*): Hello.

PAUL: You walk by here all the time –

LIZZIE: That's right. It's my lunch hour.

PAUL (*charming smile*): I couldn't help noticing, you never seem to look at us.

LIZZIE: Oh, I look a bit . . . (*She glances across at all the girls around the pool.*) But I don't tend to stare . . .

PAUL *looks at her carefully, her fearless manner. She is obviously a local girl, speaks with a Staffordshire accent. She has a natural brisk confidence about her.*

PAUL: You want to come in?

They have both moved a little along the path, there is a gap in the hedge with a clear view of the house.

LIZZIE: Not today, thanks.

PAUL: I am Paul, Paul Reynolds, by the way.

LIZZIE: I know. (*Indicating the big house.*) And that's your home. I know that too . . . (*She looks across at the estate, the surrounding fields and woods.*) And these are all your grounds, as far as you can see. But this is a right of way isn't it? I'm all right here, aren't I?

PAUL: Of course. You are free to go anywhere on my land, whenever you want.

LIZZIE: Thanks . . .

PAUL: And you are . . . ?

LIZZIE: Lizzie, Lizzie Thomas. I work in an estate agent, (*Pointing back down the path.*) in Ashbourne. So I know all about your property . . . (*She smiles.*) I should say properties . . . I read about you buying this building and that building . . .

PAUL *watches her, intrigued by her capable efficient appearance.*

PAUL: And are you going anywhere particular every time you come along here? Or are you just walking?

LIZZIE: A bit of both.

PAUL *steps through the gap in the hedge, standing almost on the path.*

PAUL: You don't want a drink? Or a little food? . . . Or a job?

LIZZIE (*politely*): No thanks. None of those.

PAUL: Not today? . . . But maybe? (*He smiles.*) I have a
selection of possibilities –
A fractional pause.

LIZZIE: I have got to go, if I want to finish my walk. I can't
be late back for work.
*She sets off, continuing in the same direction she was
heading.* PAUL *watches her go down the long straight path.
We cut back to* SNEATH *watching from afar.*

SNEATH: Will she look back? (*He watches* LIZZIE *move away
from them.*) I bet she doesn't look back . . .
LIZZIE *disappears out of sight without looking back.*

INT. ESTATE AGENT. LATE AFTERNOON
*The sound of typewriters, relentlessly loud. We are in a small
provincial estate agent. Four typists are sitting in a row typing
remorselessly; one of them is* LIZZIE. *They are under the watchful
and rather lewd eye of* MR ZACK, *a heavily-built middle-aged
man with a moustache. In the front of the office, a plump
woman in her fifties is dealing with the customers.* MR ZACK
is patrolling the typists, smoking as he does so.

MR ZACK: No slippage . . . no slippage today, girls. All
of our W's are in the right place are they? All our
Rs nice and perky, are they? (*He comes up behind*
LIZZIE *with a crude wink.*) No keys getting stuck . . . ?
All our Fs and Ks in good order?! I don't want any
slippage . . .
MR ZACK *blows smoke and moves on to one of the other
girls.* LIZZIE *stares out at the High Street, people
scurrying along the dull little street of glum shops, their
bodies hunched against the wind. The light is closing in.*
LIZZIE *types furiously.* MR ZACK *is leaning close to one of
the other girls.*

MR ZACK: I think we have a tiny bit of slippage here
haven't we . . .

LIZZIE *looks up again, as if she is expecting to see
something. The people on the street are struggling to raise
their umbrellas in the wind. She types even more
relentlessly. We stay on her face. She looks up again
abruptly as if she senses she is being watched.*

PAUL *is standing leaning against the glass window,
staring in from the street. He smiles and beckons her to
come.* LIZZIE *pauses for a second, then gets up.*

LIZZIE (*as she passes* MR ZACK): I know this customer.

MR ZACK: Mrs Wheeler will deal with the customer, thank
you very much!

LIZZIE *ignores this.* PAUL *is standing in the doorway to
the street, passers-by are scuttling past, battling against the
wind.*

LIZZIE: What are you doing here?

PAUL: Come and work for me . . .

LIZZIE (*immediately beady*): As what . . . ?

PAUL: As my secretary. (*He smiles casually.*) At first . . .

LIZZIE: At first? That sounds dangerous.

PAUL: No, it doesn't. It's exactly what it seems. Personal
Assistant. I need one.

LIZZIE *studies him, trying to work out if he is serious or
just a rich man larking around.*

LIZZIE: What happened to the *selection* of possibilities . . . ?

PAUL: I need a great secretary, more than anything else.

LIZZIE: You must have loads of secretaries.

PAUL: None that I could get on with, no. At this precise
moment there is nobody.

LIZZIE: And why is that?

PAUL (*grins, unabashed*): You will see, I expect, when you
come and work for me . . .

MR ZACK: Enough chat, Lizzie, get back to work! (*To the
plump woman.*) Mrs Wheeler, see to the gentleman –

PAUL (*leaning towards* LIZZIE): What've you got to lose?

MRS WHEELER *lumbers towards* LIZZIE *and* PAUL.

LIZZIE (*suddenly*): I'll start in a month.

PAUL: That's too late . . .

LIZZIE (*politely*): That's my offer . . . take it or leave it.

EXT. THE LARGE HOUSE. DAY

LIZZIE *gets out of a local taxi in front of the large house and stands for a moment staring up at the façade. She has dressed herself in smart formal clothes. She is carrying her portable red typewriter.*

INT. THE PASSAGES AND DINING ROOM

LIZZIE *walks down a long passage towards impressive-looking doors; she can hear loud laughter, exuberant voices. The door is very slightly ajar, she pushes it open.*

She is greeted by the sight of the occupants, all seated around a long table in a massive dining room.

PAUL *is presiding, sitting in jeans and T-shirt among his guests; some are slightly more formally dressed, but most are just wearing skimpy summer clothes. There is* COYLE, *a white blubbery individual with an immensely smooth manner; the* ALBERT BROTHERS, *loud and boisterous and in their early twenties –* ALBERT SENIOR *is about a year older than* ALBERT JUNIOR, *there is a raw energy about them;* BUTTERWORTH *with food spattered down his front;* SNEATH *munching his way through a colossal helping;* REDFERN *sitting with a notebook by him. The old aristocrats are gobbling food, various other guests we recognise from around the swimming pool. Two beautiful women are sitting either side of* PAUL.

Apart from these young women, it is an alarmingly male gathering, loud confident voices, mercurial laughter. For a second they are oblivious, and then they notice LIZZIE *standing all by herself, feeling overdressed, at the other end of the large room. A silence falls.*

PAUL: Here she is . . .
SNEATH (*amiably*): And with her typewriter . . . at the
    ready!
ALBERT SENIOR: She looks the business . . .
    LIZZIE *stands, holding her red typewriter tightly, staring
    back at them all. She tries to look unfazed but she doesn't
    completely succeed.*

EXT. THE VERANDA. THE SAME DAY
LIZZIE *has set up her typewriter on a little table in the shade.
From her vantage point she can see the gardens spread beneath
her shimmering, the various characters spotted around the
garden. She slips a piece of paper into the typewriter and starts
typing.*
    SNEATH *is sitting in the shadows close to her. He is smoking
a cigar. He blows smoke.*

SNEATH: Starting already . . . ?
LIZZIE: I need to make a list. I need to know who they all
    are. I hope you are going to help me . . . (*Watching the
    two young men moving around near the garden.*) Who
    are they?
SNEATH: The Albert brothers, they are artists . . . They're
    not actual brothers, as it happens, but they think it's
    a more handy label for when they become famous . . .
    (*He blows smoke, trying out the name slowly.*) THE
    ALBERT BROTHERS . . . It's not bad actually . . .
    The camera is moving among the guests as LIZZIE *types,
    the different shapes, the vivid faces; it lingers for a moment
    by the narrow period faces of the aristocrats.*
SNEATH: Those are just a couple of old aristos, members of

the House of Lords, you don't need to worry about
them . . .

*The camera moves on, pauses for a split second on quite
an interesting little man with huge glasses.*

You don't need to worry about him either, he is not
important . . .

*We see the haze, the character moving in the glorious
garden.*

LIZZIE: Who's the next one that matters, then?

The camera probing, looking among the characters.

SNEATH: There's Neville Coyle . . . that one there . . . he's
making his name as a brilliant right-wing thinker, just
become a backbench MP, always very pale . . . baby-
smooth complexion – I call him The Blob . . . He's
one to watch!

*We see COYLE disappearing among the roses. LIZZIE is
typing everything down. SNEATH looks rather alarmed at
her ultra-efficiency. She glances up sharply for more
information.*

SNEATH: Then there is Francis Butterworth, of course.
(*Indicating the shabby academic.*) A magnificent scholar
of medieval history, who has only written one book
ever in his life . . . but another one is expected
sometime soon . . . then there's Redfern –

*We see REDFERN gesticulating, talking very fast to other
guests.*

SNEATH: He's a revolutionary, has very radical ideas
about how to teach children, how they should play
in the woods until they are at least twelve, never take
exams . . . !

*LIZZIE is typing very fast. SNEATH watching her, she
seems so different to anyone else in the garden.*

SNEATH: And then there is Graham . . . (*Indicating a tall
genial-looking man.*) He is a poet and a homosexual . . .
a quiet bloke . . . but he makes no secret of it . . .

The camera suddenly comes to rest on SNEATH *in giant close-up.*

SNEATH: And then there is William Sneath, of course, *me*! Polytechnic lecturer in English and hack columnist on the local paper . . . who for some reason caught Paul's eye, just like everyone else here – and is hoping to prosper just by being near him . . . !

LIZZIE continues to type, SNEATH *watches her commit this all to paper.*

SNEATH: And once you are on the list – it is impossible to drop off . . . (*Grins.*) In for life, it seems . . . ! Once Paul likes you . . .

We see PAUL *moving effortlessly among his guests, chatting, charming, entertaining.*

SNEATH: It's open house, whenever you want! Some of us keep a permanent pair of pyjamas here . . .

LIZZIE (*as she types*): Yes, I can see it must be difficult not to keep coming back . . . all the free food for a start . . .

SNEATH: You bet! . . . (*Blows smoke.*) He collects people that interest him and then lets them do whatever they want . . . (*Suddenly looks straight at* LIZZIE.) And now he has collected you . . .

LIZZIE: No. I am just the secretary. It is quite different . . . (*She watches* PAUL *for a second, moving in his garden.*)

INT. PASSAGE IN THE BIG HOUSE. THE SAME DAY
We cut to a photograph of a group of people in evening dress at a party in the garden, ornamental lights hanging in the background. We pull back and see there is a whole wall of these framed photographs of parties, great dinners, dances, each of them containing a gallery of politicians and other famous people of the late seventies and early eighties: comedians, film stars, etc., faces we recognise and others we dimly remember.

We see SNEATH *and* LIZZIE *in the passage,* LIZZIE *staring at this line of photos of* PAUL*'s hospitality, all these celebrities surrounding him, everybody wanting to be near* PAUL.

SNEATH: Each party is bigger than the last! (*He grins.*) You'll have to hope you are not here when he holds the next one . . .

    LIZZIE *looks up in surprise,* SNEATH *hastily adds:*

    It's a lot to organise!

LIZZIE: It looks very glamorous . . .

    She touches one of the photos, we hear the music from the party and laughter for a moment.

    Those are great decorations in the garden . . . (*Then she looks at* SNEATH.) Why don't any of his secretaries last . . . ?

SNEATH (*smiling coyly*): I wouldn't know, would I . . . ? You must give me a ring when you find out . . .

    Suddenly there is PAUL *coming along the passage. He calls out to* LIZZIE.

PAUL: Nearly there . . . !

LIZZIE (*confused*): Sorry?

    PAUL *reaches her, gives her a charming welcoming smile.*

PAUL: I meant you've nearly reached your room, where you'll work –

    PAUL *opens a door in the passage. It reveals quite a large office, full of musty nineteenth-century furniture, box files going up to the ceiling and old metal filing cabinets.*

    Will this do?

LIZZIE: Of course.

PAUL (*gently*): It's so good you're here . . .

    PAUL *moves on.*

LIZZIE (*calling after him*): When do you want me here tomorrow? When do we start . . . ? Eight-thirty . . . ? Nine o'clock?

PAUL (*continuing on his way*): There's no rush . . . There's never any rush.

INT. LIZZIE'S ROOM. LATE AFTERNOON

LIZZIE *working in her office; everything is tidy now, and there is order in the room.* LIZZIE *is wearing dark practical clothes, there is a sense that a little time has passed, maybe three weeks. From her window she has a good view over the garden, at this particular moment just* BUTTERWORTH *is meandering about on the lawn. A bell suddenly starts ringing, an old hand-yanked bell. It is coming from somewhere in the room, but* LIZZIE *can't see where. She pulls the curtain back, it's not there. She moves towards the rusty old filing cabinet, the bell gets louder. She yanks and pulls the cabinet back, to reveal a series of old servants' bells covered in dust and cobwebs: one of the bells is clanging, rasping out. As she stares at it, the one next to it begins to ring too.*

INT. PASSAGES AND LANDING. LATE AFTERNOON

LIZZIE *is moving down the passage as the bell rings out. She turns a corner, the bell immediately above the arch in front of her begins to ring, summoning her on. A voice is calling 'Lizzie, Lizzie . . . ' It doesn't sound like* PAUL *but is full of authority. The voice continues 'Lizzie . . . where are you?!'*

She reaches the door. The voice continues 'Lizzie, are you there?!' LIZZIE *knocks.*

There is the sound of muffled movement, the voice commands 'Come in.'

LIZZIE *pushes open the door to be confronted by the sight of* PAUL*'s bedroom, a rich inviting interior. There is a very large bed immediately opposite her. In the bed are two women and* PAUL. *They are all naked.*

LIZZIE *recoils. She turns away in the door.*

LIZZIE: I am sorry, I am so sorry . . . I thought somebody was calling me.

ANGELA, *a young woman of about* LIZZIE*'s age, sits up in the bed. Her manner is totally unabashed.*

ANGELA: That was me! (*She yanks a bell rope by the bed and does her deep 'Lizzie!'*) I find these old bells work really well . . . ! (*She rings it.*) What a lovely noise they make . . . !
The other girl, CHRISTINE, *laughs merrily. They are the same women* LIZZIE *saw with* PAUL *on the first day.*
   PAUL *interrupts, seemingly contrite.*

PAUL: I am terribly sorry, it is not always possible to stop Angela . . .

LIZZIE (*turning on her heels*): I will be back in my office if you want me –

PAUL: No, there's no need to go back there . . .
   LIZZIE*'s eyes narrow.*

CHRISTINE (*laughing*): What can he have in mind?!

PAUL: No, I won't be a second, Lizzie. Wait in the white drawing room . . . *please* . . . there's a nice spread there of fruit and coffee . . . I'll be out in less than a minute.

INT. WHITE DRAWING ROOM. IMMEDIATELY ACROSS THE LANDING FROM THE BEDROOM. LATE AFTERNOON
LIZZIE *is sitting on a high-backed chair, staring at the bedroom door, like a servant waiting, very still, very straight.*
   We dissolve, the light is falling. It is evening now, she has obviously been waiting some time. We can see she is incandescent with fury, but is determined to remain still.
   We dissolve again, it is twilight now.
   ANGELA *and* CHRISTINE *erupt out of the bedroom. They are both dressed now,* CHRISTINE *is combing her hair.*

ANGELA: So sorry, everything took much longer than we expected!

CHRISTINE (*looking at herself in the mirror as she combs her hair*): Which is not always the case, is it?!

ANGELA: What are the grapes like? (*She leans down near* LIZZIE *and pops one in her mouth.*) It is all clear now . . . he is ready for you . . .

LIZZIE *doesn't move.*

ANGELA: You can go in now . . .

LIZZIE *reluctantly moves to door.*

CHRISTINE: Forgive the mess we made . . . !

INT. PAUL'S BEDROOM AND BEYOND. EVENING
LIZZIE *pushes open the door,* PAUL *is standing waiting, fully dressed. A charming relaxed figure, leaning against the end of the bed. Immediately he sees* LIZZIE *he speaks.*

PAUL: That was unforgivable. I know. I am sorry. It will never happen again.

LIZZIE *is taken aback by his humble manner, but she is still furious.*

LIZZIE: So do you need me or not?

PAUL: You were sitting out there thinking I've got to get out of this . . . have got to quit . . . ?

LIZZIE: Maybe . . . Was that some sort of test? Because if it was, I really hope I failed it.

PAUL: So are you going to hand in your notice then?

There is a fractional pause.

LIZZIE: Probably not just yet. I don't know . . .

PAUL: Right . . . (*He smiles.*) We should really do *some* work before you leave . . . Let me show you something, come over here . . .

LIZZIE *hesitates, but* PAUL *has disappeared into the next room. She crosses past the bed and into his inner sanctum.*

She is greeted by a large room which is made to seem much smaller by the amazing amount of clutter which is spread all over the floor, up to the ceiling, bulging off every shelf and surface. There are papers, books, old-fashioned Meccano, shapes and constructions, other rather beautiful models, made out of wood and paper, of buildings, bridges, etc. All of these are in confused heaps surrounded by coffee-stained waste paper. And over the walls there are huge drawings of various projects including six large modern windmills.

PAUL steers his way through the mess, dodging between the models and paper mountains, as if this is second nature to him now.

PAUL: Here is everything I intend to do . . . all my plans are here . . . ! The future is in this room.

LIZZIE: The future? You can find it in all this mess?

PAUL (*grins*): Usually . . . most days. (*He turns.*) I have been lucky so far, you know, with property . . . buying this building, selling that building . . . made pots of money without ever thinking that deeply about it. But . . .

He pulls out a little geometry box, a metal silver and blue school geometry box like kids used to have. He manages to find it wedged in between several old books. He carefully opens the box.

PAUL: In here . . . (*He hunts among rulers and rubbers inside the box.*) In here is what I *really* want to do – the list of the top ten projects . . . what I plan for the next few years . . . (*He produces a thin little piece of paper.*) A whole city centre I have a great scheme for . . . many other things, not just buildings –

LIZZIE (*staring around her*): And then there are the windmills . . .

PAUL: Clearly there are the windmills . . . ! Wind power is something I am very interested in –

LIZZIE (*going close to the beautiful drawings*): And did you draw these yourself?

PAUL *nods*.

LIZZIE: They're great . . .

PAUL (*grins, staring at the windmills*): Am I Don Quixote . . . ?
Not quite sure yet!
*There is a noise coming from a large china bowl which is
on the other side of the room. The sound of movement, and
of tapping, as if something is alive in the bowl.* LIZZIE
moves slowly towards the bowl.

PAUL (*indicating mess*): I need a little help with all this as
you can see . . . somebody who will crack the whip . . .
and get it – (*He smiles.*) organised even better then it
is at the moment.
LIZZIE *slowly peers over the top of the china bowl. Her
eyes widen. There is a baby crocodile swimming in the bowl
of water.*

PAUL: And I am interested in crocodiles too . . .
LIZZIE *staring in wonderment at the crocodile.*

LIZZIE: Why?

PAUL: I will explain later . . . (*He shuts the geometry box and
smiles.*) It's only eighth on the list . . . !
LIZZIE *looks from the crocodile to the models all around
her.*

PAUL: You'll stay? Help me make all this come true?

LIZZIE (*firmly*): We'll work normal hours?

PAUL: Of course! I am not quite as lazy as I seem. We'll
work ultra-normal hours, the most conventional hours
we can find.

LIZZIE: Not too many parties?

PAUL: No parties. *Definitely* not. I don't want to hold any
more, I promise. (*Then he adds with a smile:*) Not for a
long while . . .
LIZZIE *stares down again at the baby crocodile and then
at* PAUL.

LIZZIE: Of course I'll stay.

MONTAGE, EXT./INT. DAY

LIZZIE *is coming towards us, an efficient, compact walk. She is striding towards the camera, suggesting she now knows her way around the estate. She is wearing her habitual dark clothes, which have become almost a uniform.*

We see LIZZIE *picking up little pieces of litter as she goes. She is moving through the garden, which is vivid, colourful, almost hallucinatory, full of exotic flowers, plants and shrubs. Statues and sculptures peer at her from among the flowers.*

We hear whispered voices from among the trees, hushed teasing voices keeping pace with her as she strides along the avenues in the garden.

'*She is coming, she is coming, the Secretary is coming . . . She Who Must Be Feared . . . !*'

The ALBERT BROTHERS *are smiling at her through the foliage, not unpleasantly, like naughty school-boys as they struggle to pump up an inflatable sculpture, a giant butterfly.*

We then see LIZZIE *in a huge cloud of dust in* PAUL'*s inner sanctum. She is on top of a ladder trying to pull down the files that have been stored on the top shelves and which are covered in dust.*

She glimpses PAUL *through the dust, who is watching her efforts with approval from the doorway.* CHRISTINE *is standing next to him, whispering in his ear.*

LIZZIE (*from the top of the ladder*): I thought I might make each project colour-coded . . . give it its own colour – so we will know immediately where each idea is.

PAUL: Terrific . . . (*Moving away down the passage with* CHRISTINE, *disappearing from view through the clouds of dust . . .*) A code in colour . . . that's great!
We see LIZZIE *in a different dark skirt moving through the garden with a stack of mail in her hand, looking for* PAUL. *She glimpses him through the ornamental porthole*

in the hedge of the walled garden, lying with ANGELA *and* CHRISTINE, *who are both sunbathing topless.* PAUL *is sketching them lazily.* LIZZIE *approaches them holding the pile of letters. She greets the women with a smile.*

LIZZIE: Morning.

CHRISTINE: Hi.

LIZZIE (*handing the letters to* PAUL): There are . . . eight letters from America and one from Poland. (*To* ANGELA.) Nice day.

LIZZIE *sets off back towards the house, her brisk efficient walk. As she passes an old summer-house she hears a curious rasping noise. She approaches the summer-house from which the loud rasping sounds are coming. She pushes open the door.* BUTTERWORTH *is curled up in his chair, in a tight ball: huge snores. He is surrounded by several empty wine bottles.*

He uncoils himself, startled, when he sees LIZZIE *watching him.*

BUTTERWORTH: Just got to a difficult part! In my book . . . just struggling with it, as you can see . . . Success cannot be guaranteed, you know!

We then cut to LIZZIE *in her office, with a little black and white portable television, on which the news is playing: the Toxteth riots in Liverpool, the grainy news footage looking startling inside the grand house. As* LIZZIE *works, with these harsh images playing on the screen,* ANGELA *and* CHRISTINE *are crossing the hall in swimsuits, tiptoeing in an exaggerated way.*

ANGELA (*talks in a stage whisper*): Don't disturb the assistant . . . Whatever you do don't disturb the assistant . . . !

ANGELA *and* CHRISTINE *peer in at* LIZZIE *and continue to try and bait her.*

CHRISTINE: Always working.

ANGELA: Always buried in Paul's papers.

LIZZIE (*staring at* PAUL*'s papers*): Yes, there are some really
   great ideas in here.
   We cut to the lake by the house. The ALBERT BROTHERS
   *are playing with remote-controlled boats, the two of them
   competing with each other, boisterous, but with a real
   edge. The sail-boats they are controlling are cutting
   through the water really fast, criss-crossing the lake, their
   speed increasing all the time.*
      REDFERN *is watching the two men from the other side
   of the lake; he is calling across to them.*
REDFERN: Competitive sport is going to be a thing of the
   past! . . . didn't you know?! . . . Oh yes, I'm founding
   a society dedicated to that – NOSCP . . . ! No School
   Competitions . . . (*Smiles merrily.*) You'll be hearing a
   lot more of NOSCP . . . !
      LIZZIE *is standing by* SNEATH *watching the men and
   their games, as the* ALBERT BROTHERS *yell and scream.*
   SNEATH *seems to read her thoughts.*
SNEATH (*lightly*): Don't judge them too harshly. They come
   here to play after all . . .
   End of montage.

INT. PAUL'S ROOM. DAY
PAUL *is standing with* LIZZIE *staring at his clean, light room.
He spins around, slowly taking it all in. The clutter has
completely gone, the paper mountains have vanished. All the
files are marked in yellow, blue, green, red, gold and black.
Everything is lined up in shelves depending on its colour. All the
models are colour-coded too, so are the windmills.*

LIZZIE (*in mid sentence*): . . . so you see yellow for instance
   is the wind . . . the windmills, everything to do with
   wind power . . . that's yellow . . . you can see where
   that all is now at a glance.

PAUL (*genuinely impressed*): It's magical . . . It's spectacular!
I never thought the room could look like this . . . (*To*
LIZZIE.) It's great.

LIZZIE *smiles, relieved and pleased.*

LIZZIE: So we're ready then . . . ? For the next stage?

PAUL *looks at her. He seems to hesitate a moment.*

LIZZIE: Making these things *happen* . . . ?

PAUL: We are. Absolutely. (*Then he grins at her, daring her to
show her disapproval.*) There is just one other colour
before then . . . (*He holds up a strip of spangly colour,
mauve with silver dust.*) This colour . . . !

LIZZIE: And what's that?

PAUL (*holding the mauve and silver strip*): It's my birthday in
a fortnight. I thought I would hold a picnic . . .

LIZZIE *can't stop herself frowning.*

PAUL: Come on, Lizzie. Don't look like that . . . it's not a
party . . . !

LIZZIE: No, no. You must think I am an awful killjoy –
(*Defiantly.*) which I am not . . . It's just I thought we
were going to really start . . .

PAUL: We are. I promise! After one very small, everyday
picnic . . . (*He looks across at her.*) You'll help me?

EXT. THE PICNIC. AFTERNOON

*A wide shot of a magnificent table by the lake, under the shade
of a giant cedar tree. A gold and white tablecloth, silver cutlery,
and a series of beautiful picnic hampers decorated with flowers.*

LIZZIE *is standing in the shadows.*

LIZZIE: It's ready.

*A line of flunkies are waiting by the table. One of them
rings a dinner gong which sends a rumbling noise all over
the grounds.*

We cut to the group coming towards us, moving down

to the lake, with the house behind them. COYLE, BUTTERWORTH, SNEATH, *the* ALBERT BROTHERS, REDFERN, GRAHAM *and all the other guests and hangers-on.*

There is a new addition too. ANGELA *and* CHRISTINE *are walking together, but* CHRISTINE *is pushing a strikingly beautiful young girl,* RACHEL, *in a wheelchair. The girl looks no more than fourteen.*

PAUL *is standing in the shadows watching them approach. There are some young children in the party too.*

Time cut. We see all the guests opening their hampers, like opening Christmas presents. The glow from the red lining of the hampers on their faces, their eyes shining when they see the rich contents, the lobster, the finely cured ham, the bottles of drink. Several of the guests can't stop themselves beaming with spontaneous delight.

COYLE *touches* LIZZIE'*s arm; he is clearly very impressed by the beautiful table decorations and the food.*

COYLE: You must come and work for *me* some day, you know – (*Sharp grin.*) And I promise you I am not joking . . .

LIZZIE *is watching* PAUL, *who is close to the young girl* RACHEL *in the wheelchair; he touches her hair with easy familiarity, whispering in her ear. She seems to be the latest addition to his harem.*

We cut to the small children weaving their way through the guests. We are now well into the picnic. Some of the guests are sitting on the grass, others at the table, with the lake lapping behind them. PAUL *is at the head of the table, surrounded by* RACHEL, ANGELA *and* CHRISTINE. *Everybody is eating lustily,* LIZZIE *watching the women around* PAUL. *She is fascinated rather then disapproving, but she notices their adoring looks, their seemingly fawning attitude towards* PAUL.

A large curly-haired boy of about fifteen is suddenly by

LIZZIE*'s side. This is* OLIVER. *He has an extremely
precocious manner, precise gestures, a sharp public-school
voice. He swishes a twig he has plucked from a bush as he
talks.* OLIVER *indicates* RACHEL.

OLIVER: My sister's enjoying herself . . . good luck to her!
She has been disabled from birth you know. (*They
both watch* RACHEL *laughing with* PAUL.) But look at
the rest of them, snouts in their hampers, gobble,
gobble, gobble! If you watch people eating, after a
time it's funny how truly ridiculous it seems . . . !
They both watch the guests tuck in.
They can't believe their luck, can they?
Time cut. The guests are now full of drink.
BUTTERWORTH *is singing in a tiny high voice.* COYLE
suddenly chimes his fork against his wine glass.

COYLE: A toast . . . ! Surely the time is right for the
birthday toast.

OLIVER (*whispering to* LIZZIE): The politician . . . of course
it has to be him who thinks of the toast first!

COYLE (*holding up his glass*): To Paul . . . for his great
generosity – the most lavish picnic any of us can have
ever seen! (COYLE *stands.*) To Paul – on his birthday!

BUTTERWORTH: No number! . . . Don't put a number on
it! His age, very unlucky . . . !
Guests raise their glasses 'To Paul'.

COYLE: We're all acutely aware – I think I can presume on
this occasion to speak for others as well as myself –
we're all very aware how privileged we are to receive
such hospitality, in what must be one of the most
beautiful settings in the world . . . and the chance to
make contacts, to meet interesting people – an
unbeatable combination! *Thank you, Paul.*
PAUL *smiles graciously.*

ALBERT SENIOR: We second that . . . TO PAUL – THE
MAESTRO!

ALBERT JUNIOR: The only patron we would ever accept patronage from . . . !

BUTTERWORTH (*high drunk little voice*): Hear hear!

SNEATH: I endorse all of that and more. To Paul . . . (*He lifts his glass, with great emphasis.*) I would still be on the local paper if it wasn't for you . . . I'll never forget that . . .

The characters raise their glasses again 'To Paul!', each toast more rousing than the last.

REDFERN *suddenly stands up.*

REDFERN: This is all pathetic! I'll show you how to do it . . . !

He gets onto the table, balancing precariously, and as he speaks he walks the length of the table until he is standing right over PAUL, *swaying gently.*

REDFERN: What we *should* be saying is . . . you have vision – vision beyond your years, because there are no STRUCTURES . . . no structures of any kind . . . freedom . . . dreamtime . . . day-dreams . . . and night dreams . . . SPACE! . . . the only thinking environment that makes sense . . . The young people here – *do not forget this moment!* – because I will kneel on the table before Paul . . . ! (*He tries for a second to lower himself.*) Well maybe not . . . I do not kneel before you . . . but I do *teeter* before you, Paul, and I say to you . . . you are the One and Only . . . ! And we are truly truly grateful . . . !

The characters burst into delighted applause, RACHEL *laughing and clapping next to* PAUL. LIZZIE *watching anxiously in case* REDFERN *crashes through the table.*

PAUL *is watching all this graciously, a modest smile.*

PAUL: That's quite enough of that, all of you . . . ! But thank you.

PAUL *looks across at* LIZZIE *and makes a sign.* LIZZIE *conveys the signal on to the flunkies.* PAUL *stares at his guests down the table.*

PAUL: Now I think you need waking up . . . I've bought a little present for myself . . .

Behind the trees a red London open top bus suddenly looms up, saying 'Piccadilly Circus' on the front. It is first glimpsed through the foliage and then towers over the picnic.

PAUL: All aboard . . . ! (*He throws a bus conductor's hat at* BUTTERWORTH.) You can take the fares . . .

We cut to all the guests clambering aboard.

BUTTERWORTH: Room upstairs . . . ! There's only room upstairs!

PAUL carries RACHEL up first, her arms clasped round his neck. He settles her in the front seat. The other characters follow, clambering onto the upper deck of the open-top bus. They are in exultant mood, all the disparate characters linked by a real sense of well-being, good drink and exhilaration.

We see PAUL has replaced the flunky who was driving the bus before. He now occupies the driver's seat, revving the motor, ready to move off. LIZZIE comes up to the driver's window, calling up to PAUL.

LIZZIE: You know the route?

PAUL smiles.

LIZZIE: Because of the weight of the bus, we have got to keep to the main avenue. You do understand?

PAUL: I hear you, Lizzie . . .

LIZZIE (*pointedly*): We've got to keep to the agreed route – otherwise it will get stuck.

EXT. OPEN-TOP BUS IN GARDENS. AFTERNOON

We cut to the bus moving off, BUTTERWORTH *ringing the bell and then joining the others on the top.* LIZZIE *is sitting with* OLIVER. *Right at the front of the bus is the disabled* RACHEL, *leaning over the side, her hair blowing in the wind.*

At first we see a wide stately shot of the red London bus

crossing the estate, as we hear BUTTERWORTH's *voice, high sing-song tones.*

BUTTERWORTH: Never has a bus been so full of talent . . . !
> *We cut to the top of the bus.* SNEATH *is getting up to take photos of the group, who are still in a joyful mood.*
>
> *As he does so the bus suddenly swings rapidly to the right and starts careering across the lawn.*
>
> *We cut to* PAUL *driving really fast, just for the hell of it. He too is in an exuberant mood, on a high.*
>
> *We cut back to the characters on the top of the bus as they have to duck as branches smash towards them. They find themselves hurtling through the edge of a wood. They keep having to get lower and lower in their seats to stop themselves being injured or decapitated. There are delighted yells and screams from the* ALBERT BROTHERS.

LIZZIE (*truly frightened and angry*): What the hell is he doing . . . ?!
> *The bus continues to career on, swinging the characters from side to side.* RACHEL *is at the front, whooping with joy; she seems incredibly happy, though the ride is becoming more and more frightening.*
>
> *Suddenly we see the bus is heading straight for a large oak tree. It swerves at the last minute, throwing the characters out of their seats, hurtles on for another hundred yards, and comes to a terrifying juddering halt just clear of the trees.*
>
> *There is silence for a second.*

RACHEL: That was the best bus ride ever!

EXT. THE BUS AND SURROUNDING LAWN. AFTERNOON
We cut to all the characters spread out on the grass. They are stretched out recovering, staring up at the marooned bus, which has not moved from where it came to rest. It is deeply mired in mud.

LIZZIE *is standing at the end of the bus inspecting the damage.* PAUL *is lying on the grass watching her.*

PAUL: It's stuck Lizzie . . . don't worry about it . . .
> LIZZIE *stands with the bus behind her, staring at* PAUL. *Her small figure turns back to the bus and gives it a shove, trying to free it from the mud. The* ALBERT BROTHERS *cannot stop themselves bursting into laughter at this. Nor can* PAUL *stop himself laughing at the futility of this gesture.*
>
> LIZZIE *stares back at their laughing faces.*

INT. PAUL'S ROOM. LATE AFTERNOON
It is raining heavily now. PAUL *is watching through the window* LIZZIE *and some of the other staff trying to move the bus, attempting to tow it out of the mud. A huddle of bodies is pushing, sliding and falling in the wet mud at one end of the bus while a tractor tries to pull it free at the other end, the bus's wheels spraying mud over everybody around it.*

We cut to PAUL *sitting at his desk; he is sketching a picture of* REDFERN *on the picnic table, teetering as he makes his speech of praise, his hair standing straight up in the wind like a cartoon character.* RACHEL, ANGELA *and* CHRISTINE *are also in the room,* RACHEL *sipping a drink.*

PAUL *looks up.* LIZZIE *is in the doorway. She is completely caked in mud from head to foot, all over her hair, her face, her clothes. She stands staring at him. She is clearly furious with him.*

ANGELA (*genuinely*): You look great like that, Lizzie . . .
LIZZIE: We can't move it.
> PAUL *stares at the shipwrecked bus, ghostly now in the heavy rain.*
PAUL: I like it like that.

LIZZIE: Somebody could have got badly hurt.

PAUL: I am sorry . . . I drove too fast . . . (*Then his contrite tone.*) I've disappointed you, I know . . . I've always wanted to drive a London bus . . . and I got a little carried away . . . (*Indicating* RACHEL.) but some people had fun –

LIZZIE: Of course that explains it all . . . (*She stares back at* PAUL. *A fractional pause.*) I don't belong here, do I?! . . . I really don't . . .

PAUL (*calmly*): That's exactly why I want you here . . . to bully me . . . to cause me grief.

LIZZIE*'s manner is fearless, she doesn't mind at all the women watching her as she stands caked in mud.*

LIZZIE: That's a really great job, Paul . . . ! Find *somebody else* to kick your arse –

PAUL: Not yet . . .

LIZZIE *turns to leave.*

PAUL: I *am* working . . . all the time –

LIZZIE *looks back at him in disbelief*

PAUL: – in here . . . (*He taps his head.*) . . . going over and over things, and sometimes – I just need to let rip . . . so I can start again –

LIZZIE *turns to leave again.*

PAUL: But before you go – give me one more day. There is a room you have never seen . . . (*He looks at her very calmly.*) Let me show it to you . . . Please meet me there tomorrow morning.

INT. PAUL'S ROOM. DAY

Morning light. LIZZIE *moves through* PAUL*'s inner sanctum with all the colour-coded files staring back at her. In the far wall she sees there is a hidden door that she has never noticed before. Today it is very slightly ajar, beckoning her forward.*

She reaches it and pushes it open.

PAUL *is sitting alone in a bare white room, furnished just by a desk, two chairs, and an aquarium containing the crocodile. On one of the walls there is a series of grainy photos of a row of 1960s shops; it is the only decoration.*

In front of PAUL *on the wooden table is a huge ledger, like a medieval book.* LIZZIE *remains in the doorway.* PAUL *smiles.*

PAUL: Are you going to stay over there all the time?

LIZZIE: Depends what you've got to show me . . . (*She looks across at the aquarium.*) I see you've got him a new tank.

We see the crocodile, which has got slightly bigger, staring back at her.

  LIZZIE *indicates the crocodile.*

LIZZIE: Is that what you wanted me to see? His new home?

PAUL: No . . . (*He indicates the photos.*) Look at those . . .

We see the desolate-looking stretch of shops, which are very run down.

Those shops are the first thing I bought . . . at the age of twenty-one. My father was a Dagenham car worker. I was determined not to do that . . . not to work there . . . I saw these derelict shops, all along a high street . . . I formed a consortium – I bought the lot. Eight months, seven days a week, I worked to keep the people together, to get that money . . . (*He grins.*) The whole of 'the Empire' comes from that first purchase . . .

LIZZIE goes up close to the photographs, then glances at PAUL.

LIZZIE (*sharply*): All that work and now you can drive a London bus round your estate!

PAUL (*smiles at this*): You see this big ledger?

LIZZIE: I could hardly miss it.

PAUL: And out there . . . (*Indicating back through the hidden door.*) is all the work you've done, everything beautifully colour-coded. Would you work with me to bring all that stuff out there – into here? Into this? (*He opens the big ledger whose pages are completely empty.*) Channel it into an action plan? You will know all about my finances, sit in at meetings with my financial advisers. You will see the way things are prioritised, what figures are set aside for which projects . . . You will be able to read *all* my thoughts, (*Taps ledger.*) in here. (PAUL *looks straight at her.*) Nobody has been allowed to do that before . . . And I will give you a raise. I'll double your salary.

LIZZIE *is standing at the table, contemplating him and the empty ledger.*

PAUL: Come on, why not? . . . I want to show you I can work. (*Indicates the hidden door.*) And that door will be shut – nobody will know how to find us . . . What do you think?

He looks at LIZZIE, *waiting for a response. Silence. Then* LIZZIE *smiles slightly.*

LIZZIE: And you will tell me about the crocodile?

PAUL: Maybe . . .

Time cut. Evening light. We cut to the aquarium. It has got larger and has changed colour. Pink light inside. The crocodile is slightly larger too.

The room is full of cigarette smoke. PAUL *is poring over the ledger, a cigarette in the corner of his mouth. He is writing in a rather beautiful copper-plate. Opposite,* LIZZIE *is typing on a new typewriter. There is an atmosphere of intense concentration, of them working as a team.*

PAUL: Coffee . . . ! (*Holding out his mug sideways while still concentrating on the ledger.*) Get me some coffee.

LIZZIE *is sitting directly opposite him at the desk.*

LIZZIE: Since you're working . . . I will.

LIZZIE *moves over to make coffee in the corner of the room.* PAUL *looks up from the ledger and watches her.*

PAUL: One day Lizzie . . . you will run a major corporation.

LIZZIE *turns from the coffee, very surprised. Then laughs.*

LIZZIE: Oh yeah!

Time cut. We cut to the crocodile, the aquarium has changed again, it now stretches along half the wall. Inside it has little ferns and midget palm trees and a miniature waterfall. The crocodile is again slightly bigger.

It is night. LIZZIE *is typing and* PAUL *is working on the ledger, but the hidden door is open.* ANGELA, CHRISTINE, *and* RACHEL *in the wheelchair, are sitting in the bigger adjoining room, waiting in the shadows.*

PAUL (*without looking up from the ledger*): Whisky . . . ! (*Holding out glass.*) Whisky . . . Get me some whisky . . .

LIZZIE *gets up and takes his glass over to the corner of the room where there is now an array of bottles, a whole bar, in fact.*

PAUL (*indicating the waiting women*): You don't approve, do you?

LIZZIE: It doesn't worry me, if that's what you mean. It's none of my business.

PAUL *chuckles at this diplomatic reply.*

LIZZIE: But I thought we were always going to keep that door closed.

PAUL: Quite right . . . ! (*He looks down at the ledger, about two-thirds is now filled.*) Computers – I should buy a computer . . . but I don't like them . . . ! Get into computers Lizzie, don't let the blokes make it their preserve . . . (*He watches her.*) You know in the early days of computers, not so long ago too, there were lots of women – they understood them better than men, because it was considered as lowly as typing . . .

LIZZIE *very intrigued by this, wants to hear more. But* PAUL, *who has been glancing over at* RACHEL *through the door, suddenly gets up, and with a relaxed grin moves out of the room.*

PAUL: I'll be back in forty-five minutes . . .

> LIZZIE *stares at the crocodile. Large close-up of the crocodile's yellow eyes. The crocodile and* LIZZIE *exchange a knowing look.*
>
> *Time cut. High shot of the room, in mid-afternoon sun.* PAUL *has the great ledger open, writing one last phrase. He suddenly shuts it with a bang.*
>
> LIZZIE *looks up.*

PAUL: I think we're there . . . ! The future is planned. (*He turns the ledger towards her on the table.*) And what's more it's costed! We've finished.

> LIZZIE *stares down at the ledger and then at* PAUL.

LIZZIE: Not quite. (*She smiles.*) You haven't told me about the crocodile.

PAUL (*he grins*): I will . . . (*He taps the ledger, his tone much more serious.*) and I want to hear your opinion of all of this . . .

> LIZZIE *looks pleased.*

PAUL: But first we must celebrate –

LIZZIE: Must we?

PAUL: I have had this house for five years . . . (*He smiles boyishly.*) You've been here nearly a year . . . That must mean – it's time for a party!

LIZZIE: I wondered when that was coming . . . A small party?

PAUL: No. I am going to invite absolutely everybody I know.

LIZZIE: We'll need the whole county to house that lot –

PAUL: No. We will draw the list up together. Once it is agreed, nobody will be added. I *promise*. Don't look so serious, it's just a party, Lizzie . . . !

INT. KITCHEN. DAY

We cut to all the staff of the house lined up in the big kitchen, the cooks, the maids, the flunkies. LIZZIE *is facing them all, in her customary dark clothes. She is holding a clipboard and ticking off items as she covers them. We join her in mid-sentence as she addresses the staff.*

LIZZIE: . . . now you all know where you are going to be, you've got your positions – so keep to them. Don't wander off . . . concentrate all the time. (*She coughs.*) Excuse me, I have got a touch of flu . . . (*She looks up, determined.*) But I am fine . . . (*Sharp smile.*) Just don't come too close . . . ! Now, as you know, coming to this party is everybody from cabinet ministers to small children – I'm sure we will be able to tell the difference – (*She smiles.*) but just in case, there is a full list I'm putting up here, of everybody that is coming . . . (*She stares at the staff.*) It makes interesting reading . . .

INT. MARQUEE. DAY
LIZZIE *is moving among the gilt and white chairs in the marquee as flunkies begin to lay out the buffet.* SNEATH *is standing on the other side of the marquee. He comes towards her, giving her a little kiss on the cheek. He stares at her clothes.*

SNEATH: Lizzie, you can't wear that . . . !
LIZZIE: Why not? I'm one of the staff. I'm not a guest.
SNEATH: Don't be stupid, don't be really idiotic! You run this place . . . (*He smiles at her.*) Go and put something great on!

EXT. THE PARTY. THE LAKE. EVENING DIPPING INTO NIGHT
We cut to a ravishing image of illuminated boats in the shape of swans, drifting on the dark water of the lake. There are lights in

*the trees all around the lake. And on a pontoon floating near
the middle of the lake is a band of musicians playing. In the
glowing swans are some children and in another one is the poet*
GRAHAM, *who is laughing with the children, as they glide past
each other. Everything seems serene.*

LIZZIE *is standing watching. She has changed into a red
dress.* SNEATH *suddenly appears by her side, large drink in his
hand.*

SNEATH: Wonderful sight, isn't it?! And you look wonderful
too – now.

LIZZIE *smiles at this.*

SNEATH: The party to end all parties!
*They stare at the special lights that are all over the
grounds.*
He has designed everything himself, hasn't he . . . ?
(*Watching the guests illuminated by the special lights.*) He
really has turned into Gatsby! And you've arranged
everything brilliantly Lizzie.
*They both glance down towards the marquee where they
can just glimpse* PAUL *surrounded by people wanting to get
close to him, to engage with him, to be noticed by him.*

LIZZIE: Thanks.

SNEATH: Oh God, five bishops, three members of the
Cabinet at least! (*Smiles.*) And I don't need to tell you
who everybody is any more . . . (SNEATH *staring
fascinated at the famous people.*) I better get over there,
hadn't I, and do myself some good – it's too perfect
an opportunity . . . Got to tuck in!
SNEATH *lurches off towards the marquee. As he does so,*
LIZZIE *sees something that immediately makes her tense.
A line of vehicles, clapped-out cars full of young people,
and motorbikes with more kids on them, are pouring down
the drive.*

LIZZIE *moves off hurriedly.*

LIZZIE *reaches the metal gates that are the entrance to the party at the side of the house. The gates are being manned by tall flunkies in dinner jackets, more elegant than bouncers.*

Heading towards the metal gates, trying to get into the party, are a cluster of youths, both male and female, bikers, kids in jeans, a jumble of early eighties fashion. They are being led by the ALBERT BROTHERS, *who are in dinner jackets but with brightly coloured waistcoats covered with a pattern of naked girls.*

ALBERT SENIOR (*as he reaches the gate*): Make way . . . Make way for the unemployed . . . !

LIZZIE *stands barring their path, with the flunkies behind her. She confronts the* ALBERT BROTHERS *with an icy control.*

LIZZIE: Could you get all of these people out of here please. At once. They are not coming in here. They are not on the list.

ALBERT JUNIOR (*pushing his face close to the metal gates*): Oh really . . . !

Suddenly PAUL *appears behind* LIZZIE *and immediately beckons the* ALBERT BROTHERS *and all the kids in.* LIZZIE *turns astonished.*

PAUL: Come on in, you're all welcome.

The kids begin to pour past LIZZIE *as she stares startled at* PAUL. *He smiles at her.*

PAUL: Don't worry, this is a party for everyone. (*He grins at* LIZZIE.) It'll be fine . . . My parties need a surprise element to keep them fresh.

LIZZIE *turns to reply, but* ALBERT SENIOR *suddenly pushes through the gate and stands in front of her.*

ALBERT SENIOR: We're past the gate-keeper! Everybody in? (*He leans close to* LIZZIE.) We'll see *you* in a minute.

ALBERT JUNIOR: And you won't have to look for us, I promise.

LIZZIE *moves off. She can see* PAUL *in front of her, being greeted sycophantically, adoringly, as he mingles with his guests. She has to reach him. She is just gaining on him when* COYLE *and* SNEATH *appear and surround her. Both of them are smoking cigars, and they are accompanied by a clump of other white-faced balding men, all old before their time, middle-aged, avuncular, fleshy political types.*

COYLE: You just missed a very senior cabinet minister, Lizzie . . . there he goes! (*He indicates a disappearing figure in the crowd.*) I was hoping to introduce you . . .

LIZZIE *is eager to get past them, to reach* PAUL. *But they block her way.*

SNEATH: I was just going to arrange a time to do an interview with him, I'll take him out to lunch . . . (*Staring about him eagerly.*) plenty of good pickings to be had here . . .

COYLE (*showing off to* LIZZIE): Now we have got the Falklands back he won't be around for too long anyway . . . !

All the fleshy bald men giggle knowingly.

Lizzie, remember my offer? . . . Our agreement? . . . She is a PA made of gold, gentlemen . . . a supreme diamond . . .

We cut to the lake, the swan-boats gliding, all the lights glowing. Some of the gate-crashing kids suddenly swarm down the side of the lake. They pile into some empty swans that are tethered at the side of the lake. They immediately set off dangerously, paddling furiously, cutting through the water, smashing into each other's boats, making the ones the original guests are in wobble perilously. The kids stand up in the swans, yelling raucously.

We see LIZZIE *weaving her way through the crowd. She can see the back of* PAUL*'s head disappearing again amongst the guests. And then she sees him making for the walled garden. She follows him down one of the paths,* *calling after him. There is a crowd inside the walled garden, all the entrances are blocked.* REDFERN *is standing with* OLIVER, *the big boy, who is holding a sparkler. Everybody is watching.*

REDFERN: Ask him anything . . . ! This boy is the cleverest person at this party . . . Oh yes he is, without a doubt! Ask him anything you can think of, however obscure – he will know . . . he is like Mr Memory . . . !

PARTY GOER 1: How tall is the Archbishop of Canterbury?

OLIVER: The Archbishop of Canterbury is very tall. I think over six foot three . . .

PARTY GOER 2: And what is the biggest fish in the sea?

OLIVER: The biggest fish in the sea is the whale shark, which is known to be forty-six foot.

Somebody calls out 'What is the third largest city in Nigeria?' . . . 'What was Thackeray's first published work?' . . . 'On what day of the week did Queen Victoria become queen?' . . . OLIVER *is holding a sparkler in front of his face and stares at it intently as he answers the questions.*

OLIVER: The third largest city in Nigeria is Ibadan . . . William Makepeace Thackeray's first ever published work was *The Irish Sketchbook* . . .

As soon as the first sparkler has gone out, OLIVER *lights a second one, his dead-pan moon-shaped face staring at the sparkling light.*

LIZZIE *just catches a glimpse of this; people's backs are blocking her view.*

We see the party through her eyes: it has become hallucinatory, viewed through her heightened sense of unease and through her fever. She can only catch glimpses of PAUL *as he weaves his way through all the people at his party. He keeps disappearing.*

LIZZIE *feels real urgency about reaching him as she senses the atmosphere of the party darkening.*

She can see the raucous kids on the lake. A swan has become capsized, and another is floating upside down.

LIZZIE *quickens her step. She goes down a grassy path.* RACHEL *is sitting in her wheelchair, surrounded by other young people.*

LIZZIE (*urgently*): Have you seen Paul . . . ?! I have to find out if he needs me to do anything about those kids.

RACHEL *looks gloriously beautiful in her party dress, very sexual, but so young.*

RACHEL: He was just here . . .

LIZZIE *is immediately moving off again down the path.*

RACHEL: I wouldn't go down there if I was you . . .

LIZZIE *moves down the path. She begins to run. The path is lit by glowing white light along the grass, little footlights.*

LIZZIE *turns the corner. She is confronted by the* ALBERT BROTHERS *and some of the other kids who are sitting on a series of large aggressive-looking go-karts, like early versions of quad bikes. The vehicles form a threatening column, all of their engines are revving.*

ALBERT SENIOR: She has found us . . . !

ALBERT JUNIOR: You didn't know these were here, did you . . . !?

ALBERT SENIOR: OK! Guys! Let's roll!

The engines rev louder. ALBERT SENIOR *stares straight at* LIZZIE. *She realises as she stares at the column that there is nothing spontaneous about these kids, it was all planned in advance.*

LIZZIE: Paul arranged this with you, didn't he?

ALBERT SENIOR: Out of the way . . . *We're going to have a little fun . . . Run over a few cabinet ministers . . . !*

They ride past LIZZIE *and disappear down one of the formal avenues, the vehicles disappearing into the night, their tail-lights shining threateningly.*

We cut to the kids roaring through the formal flower garden and along the gravelled paths on their bikes,

*scattering guests in all directions, and whooping with
delight as they do so. A statue's head is sliced off, almost as
if it has been slashed with a sword.*

We cut to LIZZIE *moving among the crowd, people
swirling round her, trying to find* PAUL. *She is pushing her
way through the marquee, she asks one of the flunkies:*

LIZZIE: Where is Paul? . . . I must find Paul . . .

*She sees all the guests drinking and laughing and the kids
screaming on their bikes through the gardens, chewing up
the lawn and the flowerbeds.*

INT. MAIN HOUSE. NIGHT

LIZZIE *reaches the main house. There are guests draped all
along the staircase. She goes through a dark billiard room where
people are having sex in the shadows, and then she starts to
run down one of the long passages, past a couple of children in
party clothes, and she is just turning a corner when she comes
across* BUTTERWORTH. *He is standing in the middle of the
passage licking one of his fingers.*

LIZZIE: Have you seen Paul?!

BUTTERWORTH (*a little unsteady on his feet*): Chemical
substances have no effect on me . . . no drugs make
any difference . . . I am what I am! . . . Nothing can
change that . . .

LIZZIE *moves past him. She sees through a door into a
room where people are snorting cocaine, and right in the
shadows at the back of the room she thinks she can make
out somebody shooting up, but they are just shapes, quick
images caught though people's backs, their arms, the place
is so cluttered.*

BUTTERWORTH *appears behind her, staring into the
drugs room.*

BUTTERWORTH: I know a couple of bishops who really love this room.

LIZZIE moves up the stairs to the first floor of the house. She catches a glimpse through the window of the kids roaring their heavy bikes up to the house and right into the conservatory.

SNEATH is coming towards her as she reaches the top of the stairs. He immediately sees how agitated she is. He catches her arm.

SNEATH: Lizzie? . . . Lizzie? What's the matter?!

LIZZIE: Those kids have gone mad . . . they are doing terrible damage! Somebody has got to stop them . . . (*Then bitterly.*) They're not unemployed kids off the street! . . . They're *hired* trouble-makers – he's paid them to perform . . . !

SNEATH: It's just them larking around. Lizzie . . . You've got to calm down – Paul sometimes likes to stir up the great and the good . . . It's not as bad as it looks!

LIZZIE pushes past him, SNEATH tries to catch hold of her again. He entreats her.

SNEATH: Lizzie – just go out and enjoy yourself! . . . PLEASE!

LIZZIE is away from SNEATH. She is moving along the main landing. Suddenly she stops and stares down through the window. Two of the kids are pushing RACHEL in her wheelchair extremely fast along the side of the swimming pool. They are really running, the wheelchair is skidding along. They are yelling and shouting and RACHEL is holding on tight. It is difficult to tell whether she is thrilled or frightened.

LIZZIE watches this with alarm. But suddenly she sees something which completely galvanises her. Some of the kids are chucking paper from out of the window of the inner sanctum down onto the people below. LIZZIE sees floating in the pool are some of her colour-coded files, the pages scattered over the surface.

And now, at this very moment, slowly descending from the window as if in slow motion, is the great ledger itself. It splashes into the water and begins to sink unceremoniously to the bottom.

LIZZIE *is horrified to see this.* PAUL *is standing in the shadows watching all this happen, and he is casually chatting away to some guests as if none of this matters at all, as if it was all some planned event, a piece of enjoyable street theatre taking place at his party.*

We close in on LIZZIE. *We see her sense of betrayal. She stares at the work scattered all over the pool. When she looks up again,* PAUL *has disappeared.*

LIZZIE *runs down the stairs and out by the pool. She kneels down by the edge and begins to scoop up the sodden paper out of the water, as people's legs and feet move past her, totally unconcerned about what she is doing.* LIZZIE *stretches for the geometry box bobbing among the papers in the pool and the ruined ledger. And as* LIZZIE *tries to rescue the papers from the water she sees something glowing red out of the corner of her eye.*

She moves to get a better view, and sees some of the kids have set a waste paper basket on fire on the lawn and are trying to put it out with soda water. Other papers are on fire, floating like glowing embers across the grass.

LIZZIE *immediately runs into her office with its window onto the garden. She dials '999'. Behind her through the window the kids are chasing the burning pieces of paper and jumping on them to put them out. They are swarming all over the lawn. A voice says: 'Emergency . . . which service?'*

LIZZIE *hesitates for a second. She sees some of the other kids roaring up on their bikes, bearing down on three young children really fast, scattering them.*

LIZZIE: Get me the police please.

EXT./INT. THE HOUSE AND THE SWIMMING POOL. NIGHT
We cut to the drive. Four police cars are heading down it
towards the house.

Then we see shots of various guests scuttling into the
shadows, a cabinet minister running with his bodyguard to get
to his car, people emerging from rooms buttoning their trousers
and hastily pulling on their dresses, drugs being stored away.

INT. THE HOUSE. THE LANDING. NIGHT
LIZZIE *is sitting in the window seat on the first floor landing,*
as all the surreptitious scurrying is going on.

PAUL *suddenly appears in front of her. He looks pale and*
shocked. It is the first time we have ever seen him angry.

PAUL: Are you crazy . . . ?

LIZZIE: Am *I* crazy?

PAUL: WHAT HAVE YOU DONE . . . ?! You can't call the
police.

LIZZIE: I have called the police.

PAUL: You've gone mad . . . do you realise *who's here* . . . ?!
Do you know who some of the guests are?

LIZZIE: Somebody was going to get hurt. I couldn't find
you. I had to do something –

PAUL: That's a lie, Lizzie . . . That's not the real reason –
LIZZIE *suddenly erupts.*

LIZZIE: Not the real reason?! . . . I see . . . And what is the
real reason . . . ?! WHAT IS THE REAL REASON? –
TELL ME!

PAUL: The real reason . . . you want something I can't give
you . . . and you can't forgive me for that . . . It's not
my fault, I can't, I don't –
He stares at her lovely red dress. LIZZIE *suddenly realises*
he thinks she put it on for him.

LIZZIE: Go on – say it . . . SAY IT, PAUL! (*Staring at him; she is incandescent.*) You really think this is about sex?! . . . You arrogant shit . . . It doesn't occur to you for one single moment does it – that not everybody finds you irresistible . . . (*She stares coldly at him.*) There was a fire. There was dangerous behaviour . . . There were children at this party . . . people were going to get really badly hurt. Somebody had to take control . . . So I called the police. And I suggest you go downstairs and talk to them. Explain away your party . . .

PAUL *stares at her.* LIZZIE *meets his look.*

LIZZIE: Don't worry – I'm already leaving. You will never see me again.

EXT. POOL AND LAWN. NIGHT

We see the guests being lined up near the pool as the police move amongst them. The guests look embarrassed and awkward.

We see the police moving through the room where the drugs were being taken, picking up evidence and putting it in plastic bags. A half-dressed girl is sitting in the corner watching them do this. She is eating a dessert very slowly.

We cut back to the bewildered guests by the pool, looking very pale and cold now. We see PAUL *amongst them. The police are searching all of them. When they reach* BUTTERWORTH *he addresses them anxiously.*

BUTTERWORTH: I'm writing a book about the English heretics . . . If I keep up my current good progress I'll be finished in about three years!

We dissolve from the pages floating in the swimming pool to early morning light.

EXT. THE LAWN AND THE LAKE. MORNING

We see SNEATH *and the boy* OLIVER *walking together in the early morning light. All over the lawn and the formal gardens is the debris of the party: the litter and the leftovers are scattered everywhere, the beautiful lights are dangling, some of them have not been switched off. On the lake* GRAHAM *is floating in his swan, softly singing to himself, he is still in his dinner jacket. Pale-faced guests are staring down from the windows of the house. There is a sense that nobody has slept.*

SNEATH: Pick something, Oliver . . . choose something to keep.

They stop by one of the decorations.

There may not be another party for a while . . .

A crane shot of SNEATH *and* OLIVER *together among the detritus of the party.*

Fade to black.

EXT. STREET. DAY

A jarring sound cut, loud street noises, cars, voices, a burglar alarm ringing somewhere. Shoppers moving along a street, a long-lens shot, blurred shapes, with a group of office girls in the foreground munching sandwiches as they walk down the street. After a moment we pick out LIZZIE, *walking behind the group of office girls. She is with another woman,* CAROL, *who is slightly younger than her.* LIZZIE *and* CAROL *are in carefree mood, laughing together, window-shopping.* LIZZIE *looks more fashionably dressed than when she was working for* PAUL, *more confident, more metropolitan.* LIZZIE *and* CAROL *pause by one particular shop, selling various eighties design accessories. They stare into the interior of the shop, a relaxed moment between them.*

LIZZIE*'s expression suddenly changes. She sees something in the reflection of the window among the blurred shapes passing* *the shop. She turns abruptly, scanning the people mingling past. For a second she sees nothing, then she thinks she makes out a familiar figure, almost masked from view, somebody who looks like* PAUL *is walking along the opposite side of the street.*

CAROL (*noticing how tense* LIZZIE *has become*): What is it . . . ?

LIZZIE: I think that's my old boss . . .

She sets off, in the opposite direction. LIZZIE*'s head is down, determined to get along the street and out of sight around the corner.*

But suddenly there is PAUL *coming towards her, now on the same side of the street, heading straight for her in the middle of the pavement. He is accompanied by another man, who is wearing a leather jacket. There is no possibility of dodging out of the way, because he is staring straight at* LIZZIE.

They reach each other.

LIZZIE: Paul . . . !

PAUL *looks at her. His manner is neither hostile nor friendly. Disconcerting in its casual politeness.*

PAUL: Hi . . . ! How are you?

LIZZIE: Great . . . great.

She looks at PAUL: *he seems different, his skin a little paler. He is wearing a long coat. He looks slightly scruffier than she remembered him, but he is still an imposing figure.* LIZZIE *is struggling hard not to show how nervous she is. Next to* PAUL *is a very shifty-looking character, with darting eyes.*

PAUL: This is my business associate Ken Tyler . . . this is Lizzie.

LIZZIE (*conscious* PAUL *has not given her full name*): Lizzie Thomas –

She nods and smiles at the man, but the business associate's eyes glance shiftily sideways, not meeting her gaze.

LIZZIE: And this is Carol, Carol Drew. She works with me.

CAROL (*smiles merrily*): Hi . . . I'm Lizzie's assistant.

> PAUL*'s eyes take this in. But he doesn't seem put out, he just stares down at* LIZZIE. *For a fractional moment there is an edgy pause.*

LIZZIE: They say you never bump into people in London . . . people you know, in the street –

PAUL: But apparently you do –

LIZZIE (*nervous smile*): So I think we've disproved that . . . !

> PAUL *continues merely to stare at her. There is another edgy moment.*

LIZZIE: Are you living here now . . . ?

PAUL: On and off. (*Abruptly.*) Got to go, Lizzie . . . we have a meeting . . .

> *His* BUSINESS PARTNER*'s shifty eyes flick.*

PAUL: We're late . . .

LIZZIE (*it suddenly comes out of her*): And you're never late, are you Paul . . . ? Hate to keep people waiting . . . !

> PAUL *gives her a polite but icily distant nod, and moves off with his business partner.* LIZZIE *is almost shaking after he has gone.*

CAROL: That's him?! (CAROL *is excited.*) That was HIM?!

LIZZIE: Don't look back . . . Don't *stare*, Carol! . . . come on, just walk. (LIZZIE *sets off briskly.*) Just WALK, Carol!

CAROL (*still very excited*): It's not the first time you have seen him is it? Since . . . ?!

LIZZIE: Yes . . . I never thought I would see him again.

> CAROL *cannot stop herself staring back,* PAUL *is walking away down the street.*

CAROL: He didn't go to prison did he – for drugs? . . . After what happened? I thought I read somewhere –

LIZZIE: No, no! His guest list shrunk rather dramatically of course – for his parties . . . I'm sure he's doing OK now . . .

*She cannot stop herself looking back at the receding figure
of* PAUL. *Just as she is about to look away, he looks back at
her. A disconcerting look. Their eyes meet. We fade to black.*

EXT./INT. TAXI. DAY
We cut to SNEATH *in the back of a taxi, looking a little more
affluent than when we last saw him. He has a distinctly more
coiffured look. While the previous scene had a wintry feel,*
SNEATH *is wearing a smart summer suit. He is writing in a
large notebook balanced on his knee as the taxi travels, glancing
up when the taxi pauses in traffic and vibrates uncomfortably.*

SNEATH: I used to be able to write in cabs . . . but now
they all shake . . . !
The second time the cab pauses and shakes violently,
SNEATH *looks up in real annoyance, and as he does so he
catches sight of a dark shape through the window.*

*They are passing some playing fields on the edge of a
little urban park. Walking along on the other side of the
football pitch, glimpsed through the wire fence, is* PAUL,
with two other figures.
SNEATH: Good Lord . . . ! It *is* him . . . !
The taxi lurches on.
No, slow down, please, slow down . . . could you *just
slow down for a moment.*
The TAXI DRIVER *grumbles, the taxi slows,* SNEATH
stares fascinated out of the window.

PAUL *is striding along, and in his wake, following a few
steps behind, are* BUTTERWORTH *and the boy* OLIVER.

SNEATH *smiles to himself as he watches them. The three
figures begin to go up a sloping path in the park, and for a
moment they are silhouetted against the sky.*
SNEATH: Who would ever have thought *they* would be with
him, still . . .

We stay on the figures going up the path, PAUL *walking with determined strides,* BUTTERWORTH's *eccentric sprawling walk, and* OLIVER *fiddling with a twig and talking to himself.*

They all seem to be in their own worlds.

We fade to black.

INT. LIZZIE'S OFFICE. THE VENTURE CAPITALISTS. DAY

We cut to LIZZIE *at her desk in her mid-eighties office. The whole office floor is full of inappropriate décor, trying to suggest the firm is in touch, at the cutting-edge. It has a fruit machine in the middle of the passage, a table-tennis table, etc.*

LIZZIE *is sitting in a little glass-partitioned office. In the background we can see staff working. Some with their first personal computers and others with large electric typewriters. It is a moment of transition.* LIZZIE's *clothes continue to be fashionable, there is a hint now of power-dressing.*

LIZZIE's *phone rings, she immediately picks it up.* PAUL's *voice.*

PAUL: Hello, Lizzie . . . ? It's Paul.

LIZZIE (*startled*): PAUL . . . !

PAUL: What're you doing?

LIZZIE: What am I doing? You mean now . . . ? I'm working –

PAUL: I am round the corner. Come and meet me for lunch.

LIZZIE (*very startled*): Paul . . . I can't, I have a meeting –

PAUL (*his tone very pleasant*): Of course you can. I have been meaning to ask you to lunch. Ever since we met in the street.

LIZZIE: That was eighteen months ago, Paul . . .

PAUL (*soft laugh*): I've been busy . . . I'm in the Queen's Head, 81 Waterloo Road.

LIZZIE: That's hardly round the corner! And I can't come, I have to go to this meeting, it's important –

PAUL: Come on Lizzie, you'll just keep wondering about it
    if you don't come . . .

EXT. STREET. DAY. INT. PUB
LIZZIE *moving along a shabby, dismal street in Waterloo,*
approaching the pub. There are road works, big clouds of dust
pouring round the street. LIZZIE *walks through the dust. It is as*
if PAUL *has chosen the least salubrious place possible to meet.*

   LIZZIE *stops when she reaches the pub, pausing for a*
moment, steeling herself.

   We cut to PAUL *in the shadows inside the pub, sitting in a*
corner seat. We see him glance through the window watching
LIZZIE *hesitate.* LIZZIE *turns to go for a second and then forces*
herself to move towards the pub.

INT. PUB. DAY
We cut to LIZZIE *coming through the door of the pub, into the*
grubby interior. It is a reminder of what pubs were like in the
1980s, *the original Edwardian fittings stained with cigarette*
smoke and immensely tatty, a brutal red carpet. Through the
door can be glimpsed a lunchtime stripper doing a desultory act
for a group of pale-looking men. Everywhere is smothered in
heavy cigarette smoke.

   PAUL *is in his corner seat, two drinks on the table in front*
of him. Her drink is already there and waiting for her. PAUL
is elegantly dressed, but his clothes are very different to those he
wore in the big house. Far more subdued. He looks very pale, as
if he has not been sleeping well.

PAUL: For a moment I thought you weren't going to come
    in.
LIZZIE: For a moment I wasn't . . .
PAUL: I ordered you a drink. (*He smiles.*) I presumed . . .

You used to drink this. (*Then anxious.*) Should I get you something else . . . ?

LIZZIE: No, this is great. (*She sits.*)

PAUL: No need to be nervous.

LIZZIE (*not very convincing*): I'm not nervous . . .

PAUL: How's the job? The venture capitalists? Are they performing well?

LIZZIE: It's interesting. Could hardly fail to be really . . . trying to guess the future, back winners . . . be ahead of events –

She looks through the door at the fleshy pale men and the flabby stripper, and through the window at the road works.

LIZZIE: And this is an interesting place to choose to have lunch, Paul . . .

PAUL: Yes. I come here often.

LIZZIE *cannot be sure if he is being serious or not.* PAUL *suddenly moves very close to her, fixing his eyes on her.*

PAUL: I was an arrogant shit when you worked for me . . . But you know success, like some lousy rock star, that's what it was, it was so predictable, went to my head . . . you lose touch with who you were . . . because you can't quite believe what's happened to you . . . it's like you HAVE to behave like that . . . (*He stares at her, very humbly, very sincerely.*) I'm sorry. I'm truly sorry.

LIZZIE *is completely taken aback.*

PAUL: What's the matter . . . ?

LIZZIE: No, I'm just surprised . . . I wasn't expecting that.

PAUL (*lightly*): You can go now. If you want . . . (*He smiles.*) The exciting bit is over . . .

LIZZIE *smiles at this.*

LIZZIE: I feel, you know . . . if anybody should be saying sorry –

PAUL: Don't even start . . .

LIZZIE *is very tense, she doesn't want to get emotional,*
but she wants to respond, to make it all right.

LIZZIE: I had flu that night . . . the night of the party –
everything was so *intense*, so chaotic –

PAUL (*lightly*): Maybe that's the real reason why all sorts of
things happened – you know, in history, Napoleon,
Hitler, because they were unwell that particular night,
had toothache –

LIZZIE: So you *are* still angry with me.

PAUL: Absolutely not, a-hundred-percent not.

LIZZIE: I talked to the press, I thought you'd never ever
forgive me for that . . . I was upset –

PAUL (*breezily, magnaminously*): It's in the past. It's *gone!*
Completely gone, Lizzie.

LIZZIE *is taking big gulps of her drink; she wants to*
believe PAUL, *but she's still nervous. There is scattered*
applause for the awkward stripper. PAUL *indicates the*
vivid faces of the old men in the smoke-filled pub.

PAUL: If you think about it, pubs haven't really changed
for the last sixty years. Look at it . . . ! They should
become much more feminine, don't you think? . . .
The feminisation of pubs . . . soft lights, pink lights –

LIZZIE: I should pitch that at work, shouldn't I! (*She takes*
another big swig of her drink.) I often think of you at
work – because you were right of course . . .
computers . . . we are just getting them now . . . and
I wish I knew more than the guys about how they
work! (*She grins.*) Wind-power . . . not quite so big at
the moment, but I have read a couple of things –

As she is saying this PAUL *is taking out the same silver*
and blue geometry box, the one from his inner sanctum
that had his precious list in. He opens it carefully,
producing some money out of it, some loose change.

PAUL: Another round?

LIZZIE *is staring at the box and then at* PAUL. *The sounds from the pub are cutting out. She watches him carefully close the geometry box, she looks at* PAUL. *His calm elegance, his much softened manner, his new pale vulnerability. And she stares at the geometry box that was so full of ideas when she worked for him.*

LIZZIE*'s eyes are shining, her face flushed with excitement. She has quickly to gain control of herself to stop tears appearing.*

PAUL: Are you all right, Lizzie?

LIZZIE: I was just . . . I just had an amazing thought . . . a fabulous notion . . . What are you doing, Paul, at the moment?

PAUL: This and that . . . The bastard you met in the street with me was a disaster . . . (*He grins.*) Sometimes I pick the wrong types! But I am giving one or two things a whirl . . . Lost a bit of money, but still got enough –

LIZZIE: You wouldn't . . . ? I can't believe I'm saying this – you wouldn't join our firm . . . ?

PAUL *looks up. Silence.*

PAUL: They wouldn't have me.

LIZZIE: Of course they would! Nobody is better at reading the future than you . . . It'd be brilliant for us – the signing of the century!

PAUL *smiles. Pause. The sound of the horrible pub.*

LIZZIE: OK, it was a crazy idea. It's one of those things you blurt out when –

PAUL: I'd be honoured.

LIZZIE (*amazed*): Would you? Would you really . . . ?!

PAUL: Yes. It'd be exciting. Trying to pick successes. (*Self-mocking smile.*) In a more businesslike environment.

LIZZIE: Are you sure?

PAUL (*solemnly*): I am sure.

LIZZIE *stares straight at him.*

LIZZIE: You wouldn't have a problem . . . You know, your
ex-secretary . . . you know, being a sort of equal . . . ?
PAUL *smiles reassuringly.*

LIZZIE: It's a team business, Paul . . . You'd be . . .

PAUL: On my best behaviour. (*He stares straight at her.*)
I promise. I would love to be part of your set-up,
Lizzie . . .

INT. THE VENTURE CAPITALISTS. DAY
CAROL *turns by the window, beckoning excitedly to* LIZZIE.
*Some of the other secretaries are moving to look out of the
window too.* LIZZIE *walks slightly more slowly, not wanting to
seem to be too eager or too excited.*

LIZZIE *peers down at the car park below.* PAUL *is in the
process of getting out of a taxi, accompanied by two very tall
and very beautiful women – he seems to be being assisted by
two glorious Amazons. The two women are carrying a very slim
attaché case each.* PAUL *is carrying nothing.*

LIZZIE *smiles, slightly apprehensively.*

We cut to PAUL *crossing the main expanse of the office; he is
being followed by the two very tall blonde women.* MARCUS, *the
boss, a very short man, is following behind* PAUL's *progress,
trying to greet him, but failing to slow him down.*

MARCUS: So welcome, Paul . . . I will introduce you to
everybody –
But PAUL *is not stopping.*
– when the moment is right . . . ! You'll meet the
whole floor – a lot of names to digest in one go I know,
especially as we happen to have five Lauras at the
moment – we have Laura T, Laura B and a Laura W –
(*His voice falling away.*) and the other Lauras . . . I'm
sure you'll get used to everything here very quickly –
you'll be seeing them all at our meetings –

PAUL *stops very briefly but only to glance at* MARCUS *and* LIZZIE, *an enquiring look at which office he should be heading to.*

MARCUS: Through there! . . . that's your office . . . I hope it's sufficient?! We don't go in for big private spaces . . . in fact we are in the middle of a review – this whole space is under review – we have a design consultant working on it.

PAUL *disappears into the room with the two women. He closes the door. We can no longer see them.*

MARCUS (*calling after him*): We are going to have our regular Monday-morning meeting in precisely twenty-two minutes . . . see you there!

Time cut. Everybody is sitting pretending to work, but staring at the door of PAUL's *office. The door opens and one of the tall women comes out, and then sits demurely outside the office. Everybody looks up and then down at their work, trying not to look, very conscious there is still one woman in there with* PAUL.

The door opens, and the second woman comes out, with a broad smile on her face. The first woman gets up and joins her and they both cross the workplace and leave.

LIZZIE *immediately gets up and walks into* PAUL's *office. She finds* PAUL *sitting at the empty desk, staring out of the window. We see we are very high up with a view across the rooftops of London.* PAUL *greets* LIZZIE *with a friendly grin.*

LIZZIE (*lightly*): Since it's the first day, I'll forgive you.

PAUL *looks puzzled.*

LIZZIE: You're not going to have those 'assistants' escort you to work every day are you . . . ?

PAUL: Certainly not. (*He smiles.*) They just wanted to see what venture capitalists really look like . . .

LIZZIE *rolls her eyes at this.* PAUL *is glancing out of the*

window. The rooftop landscape, a different view of the city,
the gardens on top of buildings, the glimpses into other
people's offices. In one rooftop garden a man is dictating to
a young woman, a secretary, who is typing on a portable
typewriter.

PAUL: Great view . . . I like it already. (*He stares through the*
open door of his office at the fruit machines.) It's just a
pity about the décor . . .

LIZZIE: What's wrong with it? I like it . . . (*She stares at his*
empty desk.) Travelling light, I see . . .

PAUL (*pleasantly*): How did you end up in this place? Did
Coyle fit you up here? It's his sort of place.

LIZZIE *is startled by this insight.*

LIZZIE: He helped, yes. (*She looks at him.*) That was
the point, wasn't it . . . the point of you having all
those guests around, so they could become friends for
life . . .

PAUL *smiles at this.*

LIZZIE: Paul, you will come to all the meetings? I know
you're called a 'consultant' but you will come? I said
you would . . . It's important here, because –

PAUL: It's a team?

LIZZIE: It *is* a team.

PAUL *looks across at the girl taking dictation in the*
rooftop garden, as the man paces, talking, waving his
arms around. PAUL *then looks back at* LIZZIE.

PAUL: I love teams . . .

INT. BOARDROOM OF THE VENTURE CAPITALISTS. DAY
We cut to the management team of the venture capitalists.
MARCUS, *three other bespectacled youngish men,* LIZZIE *and*
PAUL, *watching a montage of several different people pitching*
their ideas for the future. They only get a few seconds before they
morph into somebody else.

YOUNG RED-HAIRED MAN: A line of soup . . . ! Farmyard,
wonderful smells, earthy, straight back to people's
childhood, a great nostalgic taste . . .
We cut to YOUNG BLOND-HAIRED MAN.

YOUNG BLOND-HAIRED MAN: A line of soup – supported by a
line of outlets . . . Italian flavours, strong colours . . .
colour and soup! Happy soup . . . soup to make you
smile and get up and go! Soup as energy.
We cut to DARK BEARDED MAN.

DARK BEARDED MAN: A seafood surprise . . . a line of
surprising seafood outlets . . . (*He leans forward
dramatically.*) Make the ocean do the talking . . . !
PAUL *is getting more and more restless as he watches this
montage. He is doodling away, doing vivid little sketches
of the people's faces.*

VERY TALL THIN MAN: Electric books – are the things to
get into . . . ! Everybody knows they will be taking
over. Reading books on screens, pocket-sized electric
books can carry at least a thousand titles in one
electric book . . . just flick a switch – one moment you
are in the middle of *David Copperfield*, you hit a bit of
a slow patch, don't worry . . . now *Portnoy's
Complaint!* You change from book to book . . . ! (*He
beams.*) Edit and mingle or mingle and edit!
We cut to a young droopy-haired blond woman (SIMONE)
with a casual, slightly bored tone.

SIMONE: : A flaky, very flaky meal . . . what I mean is, a
homemade-looking snack, that you eat walking along,
for the busy working woman. It looks like it has come
from one's own kitchen . . . A sort of English Chinese
roll, a whole range of shops selling finger food for the
successful . . . But your mother could have made it –
(*She sees* PAUL*'s eyes flick, not concealing his total lack of
interest in her idea.*) Or else, a gadget to turn the –

PAUL: Pages of your electric book?

SIMONE: That's right, when you are in bed . . . the book will be on a screen – and you flick the pages without ever having to touch any paper.

We cut to two excitable young men wearing virtual-reality headsets.

VIRTUAL-REALITY MAN (*talking with the headset on*): This is the future for entertainment . . . ! You live inside it, you select where you go. You are alive in 3D . . . ! Nobody *dictates* how the story goes, *you* choose . . . inside your own home, you can go anywhere, have any ending you like – you are the film director, you are the storyteller – you are the master . . . !

We see the management committee beaming impressed. All except PAUL.

We cut to LIZZIE and MARCUS sitting wearing the headsets, as the young men grin with enthusiasm.

VIRTUAL-REALITY MAN: Great, isn't it!

PAUL gets up.

PAUL: People *rather like* to be told stories . . .

He leaves the room. MARCUS still with the headset on, calls after him.

MARCUS: What happened? . . . Where did he go?

INT. VENTURE CAPITALISTS' OFFICE. AFTERNOON

The office staff are wearing autumnal clothes. They are working away in silence. Just one typewriter is left now, an older worker typing in the corner.

The door to PAUL's office is shut, but outside is a pile of dusty old secondhand books. LIZZIE can see a beetle crawling over one of the books. There is a strange thumping sound coming from the other side of PAUL's door.

LIZZIE walks towards the door, knocks and without waiting for a reply goes in. She is startled to see PAUL has a guest. Sitting on the floor of the office in the corner is BUTTERWORTH.

He is rocking with laughter, and pounding the partition wall with his fist for added emphasis.

PAUL (*looks up*): Anything you want?

LIZZIE: I just wondered what the noise was.

BUTTERWORTH: The noise is me! (*He beams at* LIZZIE.)

LIZZIE (*trying to smile*): Well, whatever it takes.

> LIZZIE *sees the room is now full of a montage of photos covering all the walls. There are also* PAUL's *drawings of people doing their pitches in the boardroom.*
>
> *There are two huge photo portraits of Rupert Murdoch and Richard Branson dominating the wall.*

LIZZIE: Why are those up there? (*Sceptical.*) Your heroes?

PAUL: Neither heroes nor villains . . . just a reminder of
   what not to become.

> MARCUS *has appeared behind* LIZZIE. *He is peering over her shoulder into the office. We sense his slight unease about* PAUL.

INT. MAIN OFFICE. DAY

We cut to all the staff gathered in the main office. Every glass partition has gone, there are no more individual spaces.
MARCUS *is addressing the workforce.*

MARCUS: We are restructuring as you can see – and not
   before time! Our space is now communal, no special
   desks, no ownership of surfaces. As the work happens,
   the space happens. We're all a team, a unit that lives
   and breathes in the same environment . . . as open as
   the sky –

> *In the middle of the meeting, as* MARCUS *is saying this,*
> PAUL *is sitting reading a very large and very old book. He never looks up.*
>
> *Time cut. We cut to* LIZZIE *at her desk. She looks up*

sharply, across at PAUL. PAUL *'s clothes have changed
since the previous scene, and so has his book. But he is
sitting in exactly the same position, reading and never
looking up. People keep glancing in his direction, snatching
quick looks at him, as* PAUL *carefully turns a page and
continues reading, totally untroubled. Behind* PAUL,
BUTTERWORTH *is sitting at another desk, also reading a
very old book and chuckling loudly to himself.*

MARCUS *comes up behind* LIZZIE, *a loud whisper.*

MARCUS (*glancing at* PAUL): What's this about . . . ? Why is
he being such an arsehole . . . ?

LIZZIE: I think you should give him his office back. I think
that's important to him. I mean, he is a sort of
solitary thinker, isn't he . . . that's his speciality.

MARCUS: I thought he was meant to be giving us his great
report . . . all his big ideas.

LIZZIE: Give him his office back *and he will.*

Time cut. We cut to PAUL *going through a newly
constructed partition, back to his old office. He turns and
gives a little wave to everyone before he disappears. The
door shuts.*

INT. THE MAIN OFFICE. EVENING

We cut to evening light. LIZZIE *goes up to the water-cooler. As
she bends down she has a shock. Just by the water-cooler, in the
shadows,* BUTTERWORTH *is sitting on the floor reading a book.
She hadn't seen him there at all. Behind him, snaking all the
way to* PAUL *'s office, where the door is still shut, is a long line
of dusty old books.*

BUTTERWORTH *grins and gives* LIZZIE *a thumbs-up sign.*

BUTTERWORTH: Any day now, he will be giving his report . . .

INT. MAIN OFFICE. MORNING
We cut to the main office. Everybody has gathered, there is an atmosphere of terrific anticipation.

MARCUS (*muttering to* LIZZIE): This better be worth waiting five months for . . .
  PAUL *comes out of his office. He walks calmly through all the waiting people. He pauses for a second and then sits at one of the empty desks. He has one very slim folder under his arm. He puts it in front of him, adjusting its angle on the table slightly.*
    LIZZIE *is watching him, expectantly, hopefully, quietly excited, willing him to do well.*
MARCUS (*serious, forceful*): As you know, over the last few months Paul has been working as a separate team – a team of one, you might say . . . (*Glancing sideways at* BUTTERWORTH, *who is propped up in a corner.*) which on occasions has had added members . . . but was essentially a focused project of his own. And now we are going to hear the fruits of his work – what Paul thinks should be our priorities, ideas we should be particularly concentrating on, themes we should be alive to, growth areas that are poised to explode . . . Over to you, Paul . . .
PAUL (*solemnly*): Marcus . . . thank you. I have one word for you . . . when you say it out aloud it sounds like two words, but of course it is spelt as a single word. So I have one word for you . . .
  Bookshops.
  There is an audible gasp that goes around the office. People are bewildered, not certain if this is an uncomfortable joke, or if he is being genuine.
    PAUL *repeats the word with added emphasis.*
PAUL: BOOKSHOPS!

MARCUS *looks completely confused for a second. Then he begins to shake with rage.*

MARCUS: And . . . ?!

PAUL (*innocently*): And? . . . There is no 'and', Marcus. Why should there be an 'and'? One pure idea is what you want. There are very few bookshops; a chain of quality bookshops, perhaps with a coffee shop tucked inside – that's what is needed . . . (*Suddenly loud, like a chant.*) Books and shops . . . ! And coffee! Let the books do the talking . . .

We move in on LIZZIE, *who has gone pale. At first bewildered and upset, then silently furious.* PAUL *gets up from his desk and picks up his open folder.*

PAUL: Anyone wanting more details . . . I will be available in my office . . .

He smiles at them all, and disappears back into his office. BUTTERWORTH *beams at all the staff, he is full of his own enthusiasm for* PAUL*'s announcement. Everybody else is looking at* LIZZIE.

MARCUS (*watching* PAUL *disappear, then turning on* LIZZIE): That shit! . . . That fucker! . . . I'm too angry . . . If I go anywhere near him now – I think I'll hit him . . . (*He suddenly yells.*) He got his office back – FOR THAT!!

LIZZIE *is incredibly angry, determined.*

LIZZIE: Don't worry . . . I will handle it. I promise you.

INT. PAUL'S OFFICE. DAY

LIZZIE *enters* PAUL*'s office without knocking.* PAUL *is sitting at his desk, nonchalantly reading.* LIZZIE *is trying to remain controlled, but she is too angry.*

LIZZIE: How dare you . . . HOW DARE YOU!

PAUL: What have I done?

LIZZIE: You just came here to disrupt everything, didn't you . . . ?! To humiliate me . . . ?! You promised . . . YOU PROMISED me you wouldn't do this . . . that you'd behave yourself –

PAUL (*seemingly genuinely surprised*): And I have, haven't I?! . . . I've been quiet . . . haven't ordered people around . . . haven't thrown my weight about . . . kept myself to myself . . .

LIZZIE *is infuriated by this reply.*

LIZZIE: You bastard . . . I *believed* you . . . I supported you . . . ! But you never had any intention of working properly, did you?! You didn't need this job – so you thought I'll just take the piss . . . You just wanted to belittle me in any way you could . . . Everybody knows you were my idea . . . !

She stops in mid-sentence. Something has caught her eye in the photo-montage on the wall, something which she has never seen before on PAUL*'s wall. A picture of herself and a headline from the* News of the World *from the time of the party 'Secretary Tells of Property Millionaire's Drug Den'.*

  LIZZIE *takes this in for a second, then looks straight at* PAUL.

LIZZIE: Your idea of a little revenge – to come here and then stop anybody having any respect for me at all . . . to try to make me a laughing stock –

PAUL (*quiet, calm*): I don't know what I have done . . . (*Then he can't resist.*) I thought I'd been the perfect employee . . . !

LIZZIE *is beside herself at* PAUL *pleading innocence.*

LIZZIE: Get out of here . . . *Get the fuck out of here – now!*

PAUL (*simply*): It's a good idea Lizzie, the bookshops, it really is . . .

LIZZIE: Five months' work . . . ! That's five months' work?!! It's a farce . . .

PAUL: You really want me to go?

LIZZIE: I want you out of here in the next half an hour . . .
    (*Indicating the piles of old books.*) And take all this shit
    with you . . .

PAUL: Then I'll go. I will go, Lizzie. No hard feelings –

LIZZIE: That's what you think . . . ! I just want you out of
    here, Paul . . . (*Suddenly conscious of her raised voice,
    trying to get control.*) Everybody's listening to this . . .
    Everybody is watching.

PAUL: You should get out of here too, you know.

    LIZZIE *clenches again.*

LIZZIE: I am not even going to bother to reply to that –

PAUL (*staring straight at her*): Because you really don't
    want to make a habit of destroying everything you
    touch . . .

    LIZZIE *can't stop herself responding to this.*

LIZZIE: ME?! *I* do that . . . I DO THAT, DO I?! . . . This
    was a pathetic idea of mine . . . so stupid . . . that you
    should come here . . . thinking that you could ever
    change . . . it was the worst idea of my life . . . (*She
    moves to leave and half-trips on the pile of old books.*)
    And get rid of all these horrible old books too . . .
    everything . . . just take *everything* . . . !

    LIZZIE *walks away, leaving the door of* PAUL'*s office
    open. We see the other members of staff staring towards*
    PAUL.

    We track back from PAUL *at his desk until he is a small
    figure at the other end of the office.*

    We fade to black.

EXT. ST JAMES'S, LONDON. NIGHT
*We cut to a subjective shot, we are in the middle of a group of
men in dinner jackets swirling around on the pavement outside
a London club. They have just come out of a dinner, their cars*

and drivers are lined up waiting. The power élite. We see
SNEATH *amongst them, watching everybody beadily. He sees*
COYLE *standing smoking a cigar, surrounded by the gossiping*
bald men. SNEATH *approaches him.*

SNEATH: A surprisingly good dinner!

COYLE: The pudding was good at least . . . (*He blows smoke,*
he is ambling towards his waiting car.) Did you hear the
Home Secretary saying that She could be gone soon?
. . . There are rumblings, rumblings, rumblings . . .
(*He grins.*) But you know what I think? She's only
done ten years, she wants to do at least twenty . . . !
SNEATH *stares at the men, all gossiping on the pavement*
in their tight little groups.

SNEATH: Always got your finger on the pulse, haven't you
Neville . . . !

COYLE: I try . . . (*He smiles.*) It's what I do best . . . (*He has*
the door of his chauffeur-driven car open.) Do you need
to ring home?

SNEATH (*taken aback*): Ring home . . . ? I don't think so . . .
it's not that late –

COYLE (*surprisingly keen*): Come on, surely you need to
ring home! One quick ring . . . (*Indicating the back of*
his car.) Come on, you can do it from in here . . . (*He*
smiles.) Free service in comfort!
SNEATH *at last realises* COYLE *wants to show off his new*
phone. SNEATH *sits on the back seat with* COYLE.

SNEATH: So you have got a portable . . . (*He picks it up,*
with its large heavy black battery attached.) Jesus, it's
heavy . . . you carry this around with you . . . ? It's a
monster! It's like something you might use to blow up
a block of flats . . . (SNEATH *mimes pushing a dynamite*
handle down. Then he starts to dial.)

COYLE: One really needs a manservant to carry it behind
one, doesn't one? . . . Maybe I can ask my PPS to do it!

SNEATH (*into phone*): Darling . . . I'm on a portable phone
    in the back of a car . . . just rang to say . . . I'll be
    home in fifteen minutes . . . that's all . . . nothing else!
    (*He rings off.*)

COYLE: Good isn't it?! Bet you want one . . . (*He takes back
    the phone.*) Now – I would give you a lift . . . but I am
    going in the other direction . . .
    We cut to SNEATH *running across the road, dodging
    among the West End crowds and jumping on a bus.*

INT. LONDON BUS. NIGHT

We cut to SNEATH *taking a seat on the top of a bus, among a
crowd of West End revellers, kids and tourists. He stares down
out of the window as the bus moves off at the remaining little
clusters of men on the pavement discussing the affairs of the
world, and the caterers carrying the floral arrangements from
the banquet out of the back entrance, like a column of Victorian
servants.*

*The bus travelling through the West End, different languages
ringing round the top of the bus, kids laughing.* SNEATH *sitting
contentedly in his dinner jacket thinking about his evening.*

*A voice suddenly calls softly 'William . . . ? Good dinner was
it, William . . . ?'*

SNEATH *turns startled. There, a couple of seats back, is*
PAUL. *He is casually dressed in jeans, and is unshaven.*

SNEATH: Paul . . . !

PAUL: How are you, William?

SNEATH: Pretty good . . . (*Trying not to seem too shocked at
    seeing* PAUL.) Keeping my head above water . . . ! (*He
    laughs a bit too heartily.*) Fancy seeing you on the top
    of a bus!

PAUL: I like buses. Remember . . . ?

SNEATH: Of course . . . the picnic! (*Then hastily changes the subject.*) I like buses too – I'm much too mean to take taxis all the time . . . ! (*He gets up suddenly.*) So we must catch up some time Paul, very soon . . . this is my stop now. So –

PAUL: Don't get off, William.

SNEATH (*unnerved by* PAUL*'s intense stare*): I have to get off, this is my stop, somebody is waiting for me to get home –

PAUL: Miss your stop . . .

SNEATH: Miss my stop?!

PAUL (*catching* SNEATH*'s sleeve*): There's something I want to show you . . . it's not far. Since you're here, and I'm here . . . what have you got to lose . . . ?

We dissolve to the bus passing through an urban landscape, far away from the West End.

We cut inside the bus. There are only three other people left on top of the bus. PAUL *is now sitting next to* SNEATH.

SNEATH: I thought you said it wasn't far . . . (*Nervous laugh.*) I can't believe I have agreed to do this! –

PAUL: We're nearly there . . . (*He smiles.*) it'll be worth it. (*He looks at* SNEATH*'s nervous face.*) Was he following me . . . ? Is that what you're thinking?

SNEATH: You weren't following me?! Surely not?

PAUL: I saw you with The Blob, in the back of his limo . . . (*He smiles.*) But then I could have just been passing . . .

SNEATH: Why would you want to follow me?

EXT. URBAN LANDSCAPE. NIGHT

We cut to PAUL *and* SNEATH *getting off the bus. It rolls out of shot. We see we have reached the bus depot, it looms up behind them.*

SNEATH: It's the end of the line . . . ! You've taken me to

the end of the line! . . . This is ridiculous, Paul! What
on earth are we doing here?!

PAUL: It's just a little eatery round the corner here. Best
food in London –

SNEATH: But I have just eaten! I am absolutely stuffed with
food –

PAUL: But you can *always* eat, William, can't you . . . ?
*They are passing graffiti-stained walls, dark buildings, a
sense of being on the very edge of the city.*

SNEATH: I need to call my girlfriend . . . I ought to have
one of those two-ton phones, oughtn't I?!
PAUL *indicates a little café glowing out of the surrounding
dark.*

PAUL: One of the only twenty-four-hour eateries in
London. It's amazing how few there are still . . . (*He
smiles at* SNEATH.) Inside . . . a little surprise.

INT. CAFÉ. NIGHT
We cut to PAUL *and* SNEATH *entering the stark café with its
check tablecloths and red plastic tomatoes. There are some
striking faces among the clientele. A large heavily-built young
man sitting on his own, eating without looking up – a thin-
faced rather well-dressed middle-aged man who looks like a
solicitor; a couple of lorry drivers sitting together; a small
nervous man reading Proust and eating as he reads; and a
middle-aged woman sitting on her own smoking. All of them,
apart from the lorry drivers, are by themselves.*

SNEATH: Spooky place! All that way for this?!
Time cut. We see SNEATH *biting into a large sandwich. He
is sitting opposite* PAUL, *who is just drinking a coffee.*

SNEATH: You're right, I did have room for this – and it's
good too! Mind you, you can't go wrong with a bacon
sandwich –

Lizzie entering Paul's house to become his secretary

Paul in his study with the geometry box

The Albert Brothers, as artists in the early eighties

Redfern celebrates Paul's birthday at the picnic

Sneath watching everything at the picnic

Coyle, Christine, Rachel and Angela at the start of the party

Paul's great party

Paul gatecrashes Lizzie's wedding

Paul, Butterworth and Oliver agree to leave the wedding

Lizzie arrives at Paul's farm

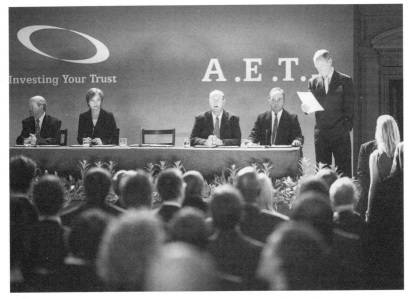

The angry shareholders confront Lizzie, Anders and the other executives

Lizzie is engulfed by the press after the collapse of A.E.T.

Paul suddenly appears at night in Lizzie's office

PAUL *is watching him.*

SNEATH: So what did you want to show me . . . ?

PAUL: That man – (*He indicates the heavy-set young man
who is in his twenties.*) Recognise him . . . ?

SNEATH (*looking across*): No . . . should I? No, I don't . . .

PAUL: Look again.

SNEATH: No, I don't recognise him. Never seen him
before.

PAUL: That's Oliver . . .

SNEATH: Oliver?! Good Lord . . . Is it really him? . . .
(*He calls across.*) Oliver!

OLIVER *doesn't look up.*

SNEATH: Oliver . . . ?!

*The young man glances up, gives one small nod of
acknowledgement, gets back to his solitary eating.*

What's the matter? . . . I'll go over – (*Gets up.*)

PAUL: No, leave him . . . he keeps himself to himself . . . If
he wants to, he will join us.

SNEATH *reluctantly sits again.*

PAUL: We both found this place separately. I have
discovered it's full of people who can't sleep . . .

SNEATH: You can't sleep?

PAUL: I find it difficult to, sometimes, yes.

SNEATH: Is it . . . ? (*Pauses for a second.*) Is it because the
money has gone?

PAUL: No, no – that's not important.

SNEATH *looks disbelieving.*

PAUL: No, it really doesn't matter to me that much. I
gambled on a few things and lost – so what? And I got
involved with the wrong people. At least it was all my
doing . . .

SNEATH *glances over at the solitary eaters, and at*
OLIVER.

SNEATH: You sure I shouldn't go over? I feel strange just
sitting here –

PAUL: Leave him . . . it's OK.

> *We see the other faces around the café.*
>
> You hear some extraordinary stories here . . . people who have been shafted by their business partners, lost their house, suddenly lost their job and are left by their wife all on the same weekend . . .
>
> SNEATH *is very unsettled by the people in the café. He decides to change the subject.*

SNEATH: Bumped into anybody else from the old days . . . ?

PAUL: You mean have I followed anybody else?

SNEATH: I don't believe you are following me . . . ?!

PAUL (*smiles*): Suit yourself. I saw the Albert Brothers –

EXT. STREET. DAY / INT. CAFÉ. NIGHT

We see the ALBERT BROTHERS *moving along a pavement. They are now much stouter, big heavy men in suits, one of them carrying the* Financial Times. *They are talking rapidly together as they walk. They suddenly glance back to see* PAUL *behind them. They give a little nervous wave of recognition before they quickly disappear into the crowd.*

> *We cut back to* PAUL *in the café.*

PAUL: They looked very straight, but rather podgy!

> *Then we see a cinema queue.* REDFERN *is in the queue sheltering his face with his newspaper, trying to make himself invisible as he shuffles in the queue.*
>
> *We cut back to* PAUL.

PAUL: I saw Redfern when I was going to the cinema . . . (*He grins.*) He started hiding . . . pretending he hadn't seen me.

SNEATH: I'm sure people aren't avoiding you –

> PAUL *smiles at this.*

SNEATH: You don't seem bitter about it?

PAUL (*calmly*): No. I find it very interesting how people
    react to seeing me . . . (*Glancing at* SNEATH.) you have
    to admit it's fascinating, especially since I introduced
    them all to each other . . .

SNEATH: And Lizzie?

PAUL (*quiet*): No. I haven't seen Lizzie.

SNEATH: She's getting married very soon. Big wedding!
    I got my invitation last week –

    PAUL *looks up, deeply intrigued.*

PAUL: Really? I haven't got mine.

SNEATH: Well she wouldn't, would she . . . ?

    PAUL *looks at* SNEATH *blankly.*

SNEATH: She wouldn't want you at the wedding for
    Chrissake, Paul! There's a feud going on between you
    two . . . Remember?!

PAUL (*quiet, intense*): There is no feud.

SNEATH: OK, if you say so . . . right! (*Suddenly worried.*)
    I shouldn't have mentioned it . . . I'll send her your
    best wishes then? Shall I – for old times' sake?

    We stay on PAUL *for a second.*

PAUL: Of course.

    Fade to black.

EXT. THE WEDDING. SUMMER. EVENING

    We are moving with PAUL *towards some metal gates
    leading to the wedding reception. Behind him, shuffling to
    keep up, are* OLIVER *and* BUTTERWORTH. PAUL *is
    walking fast, moving among the other guests as they head
    for the entrance. He is dressed in a different style to the
    previous scene, his hair in a ponytail.*

    *There is a crush at the gates as the invitations are
    checked.* PAUL *waves a card, as do* OLIVER *and*
    BUTTERWORTH.

PAUL (*airily*): The Fotheringays . . .

>*The people on the door glance down at their list, by the time they have looked up the three of them have slipped in.*
>
>*In front of them lawns stretch down to a lake and the marquee. The setting is immediately suggestive of* PAUL'*s old house and grounds. It is a different place but carrying a strong reminder of the past.*
>
>PAUL *never stops moving, dodging between the people,* BUTTERWORTH *and* OLIVER *in tow all the time.* BUTTERWORTH, *his eccentric walk, huffing and puffing, and* OLIVER *locked in a silent world of his own. All around them we catch glimpses of faces we have seen before, little twinges of recognition: there are the old aristocrats, and the* ALBERT BROTHERS, *tall and loud, stooping to hear what the other guests are saying and then laughing heartily: they look prosperous and prematurely middle-aged. We see* MARCUS, *the very short boss from the venture capitalists, and in another cluster of people is* MR ZACK, LIZZIE'*s original boss from the estate agent.*
>
>*It seems her whole life has been invited to the reception.* PAUL'*s progress is suddenly halted. The three of them pause and stare down at the lake in surprise. Gliding on the water are boats in the shape of illuminated swans, just as at* PAUL'*s party. They are painted in different colours, black and gold with red beaks, instead of white and gold. Their lights are just beginning to show.*
>
>*There are other touches that have been borrowed from his great party, including a pontoon bridge that stretches into the lake, but this bridge goes across the whole lake to the other bank. Some of the guests are walking up and down the bridge, teetering in their fine wedding outfits. From a certain angle they look as if they are walking on water.*
>
>*But there is a dominant feature, brash and loud, that is totally different from the past. A huge video screen is next*

*to the marquee, and is playing images of the reception as
people pass its camera. Guests waving at themselves. There
is loud music coming out from big speakers on either side
of the screen. Everywhere you look there is a sense of late
eighties excess, self-confidence, prosperity and celebration.*

PAUL *weaves his way through the guests, his manner
purposeful but not manic. He looks intrigued at what he
sees. We see the old aristocrats noticing him, and some of
the other minor guests from the days of the big house. He
is like a shadow crossing the reception, disconcerting just
by his presence, and his calm amused demeanour.*

*We are moving with him all the time, searching with
him for a sight of* LIZZIE.

The camera and PAUL *literally bump into the* ALBERT
BROTHERS.

ALBERT SENIOR: Paul . . . ! We haven't seen you for so long!

PAUL (*knowing smile*): Haven't we? (*He looks at their plump
prosperous appearance.*) You look very different
somehow, you two –

ALBERT JUNIOR: Sure! . . . Because we are creating
anarchy in the city now – instead of in the art world.
Got to look the part, haven't we . . . !

ALBERT SENIOR (*laughing in a self-congratulatory way*): So
we can fleece them . . . !

PAUL *is not stopping. Through the crowd he has caught
a glimpse, on the other side of the lake, of* LIZZIE. *She
is dressed in a long, white, traditional wedding dress,
surrounded by guests and little bridesmaids running
backwards and forewords. She looks radiantly happy.*

PAUL *walks across the pontoon bridge towards her with*
BUTTERWORTH *and* OLIVER *following.* LIZZIE *has not
seen* PAUL *and is greeting her guests on the far bank.*

Halfway across the bridge PAUL *suddenly bumps into*
REDFERN, *who is travelling in the opposite direction,
talking at the top of his voice to two young women.*

REDFERN *has fashionable glasses and a new cropped
hairstyle. He looks completely different, more like an
executive. He now has a slow dogmatic delivery, none of
his previous wild enthusiasm remains.*

REDFERN: Paul . . . ?! Goodness me . . . ! Fancy seeing you.

PAUL: Fancy.

On either side of the bridge the swan boats are gliding.

REDFERN: Amazing, here we all are . . . ! Together again . . . !
Older certainly . . . (*Pompously.*) Wiser . . . ? Maybe . . .

OLIVER (*muttering to himself*): Definitely not.

REDFERN: Is that you, Oliver? . . . Good lord, it is Oliver!
How tall is the Archbishop of Canterbury? (*Laughs.*)
You know I'm always holding you up –

OLIVER: Holding me up?

REDFERN: I hold you up as the cleverest child I ever saw.
And why? I will tell you why – because you took all
your exams and passed with maximum marks! I was
so wrong all those years ago . . . so very wrong. We
have to measure and define . . . always! Checking a
child's progress . . . testing and testing –

PAUL: You're a government advisor now aren't you?

REDFERN: *Chief* Educational Advisor . . . Discipline and
creativity . . . hand in hand, inextricably linked. That's
where we are! Isn't that right, Oliver?

PAUL, OLIVER *and* BUTTERWORTH *are already moving
on. As they near the end of the pontoon bridge they see
there is a group of people waiting for them on the bank.*
COYLE, SNEATH *and some other guests from the old days
stand barring their path, almost like a posse.*

SNEATH: Paul, what are you doing here? Don't cause
trouble please . . . it's Lizzie's great day.

PAUL (*calmly*): I'm here to cause trouble? What gave you
that idea?

COYLE (*taking him by the arm*): Paul, let me get you a
drink . . .

PAUL *sees* LIZZIE *disappearing amongst the crowd in her white dress. A young, good-looking man,* RALPH, *comes up to them excitedly.*

RALPH: Isn't it great that the weather has decided to be so wonderful! . . . I think we've hired the most beautiful house in England . . . and the décor and everything – looks amazing don't you think?! I can say that, because Lizzie did it all . . . Lizzie did everything! – And it's a double celebration . . . did you know that? . . . because she has just got a great new job, too . . . !

COYLE: Oh yes, she has indeed, at A.E.T. (*To* OLIVER, *patiently.*) One of the biggest companies around . . . a *good* move . . . (*Self-satisfied.*) I had a little hand in arranging that . . . (*He indicates a large, confident-looking man,* ANDERS.) I made a few introductions – that's her new boss . . .

RALPH: Yes, he didn't think he could make it, but he has! Everybody's here today! (*He moves off happily.*) See you later!

COYLE: The groom . . .

PAUL *smiles warmly.* SNEATH *gives a signal to* COYLE *to keep close to* PAUL.

SNEATH: I've got to go and get ready . . . study my little speech . . . (*Suddenly appealing to* PAUL.) Here's fine, Paul, just here by the water – but maybe not in the marquee . . . OK?!

PAUL (*as* SNEATH *leaves*): Don't worry . . . (*He glances at* COYLE.) You won't have to guard me – we'll stay rooted to this spot . . .

BUTTERWORTH *nods and sits on the grass.*

For a moment they are all staring at the water. The swans on the lake are glowing brighter now, the people inside them rowing.

There is a quick cut to GRAHAM *the poet, alone in his swan at the original party, drifting on the lake at night.*

PAUL: Graham died, you know . . . (*We cut back to* PAUL.)
Remember Graham the poet? He died of AIDS.
>   COYLE *is not sure what to say, he dislikes this shadow*
>   *crossing the party.*

COYLE: That's sad . . . poor chap . . . (*He stares at* OLIVER.)
He doesn't say much any more, does he . . . ?!
>   *We stay on* OLIVER *staring at all the faces from the past*
>   *as they loudly carouse.*
>
>   *Time cut. It is twilight. The lights have come on all*
>   *around the marquee and on the lake the swans are*
>   *drifting, fully illuminated. All the guests are sitting in the*
>   *marquee eating, finishing the celebratory meal.*
>
>   PAUL, OLIVER *and* BUTTERWORTH *approach the*
>   *entrance to the marquee, keeping to the shadows, glancing*
>   *at the reception through a flap. We see* LIZZIE *sitting with*
>   RALPH *at the centre of the table, surrounded by flowers,*
>   *with* SNEATH *next to them as the best man and* COYLE
>   *near* LIZZIE *too.* SNEATH, *thinking* PAUL *has left, is*
>   *looking much more relaxed. He stands up and taps the*
>   *microphone.*

SNEATH: Any moment the speeches will be descending, so
scrape those plates . . . Lick those bowls . . . !
>   *As* SNEATH *is saying this* LIZZIE *suddenly looks up and*
>   *sees* PAUL *for the first time. She goes pale, immediately*
>   *stops talking, their eyes meet. Then* LIZZIE *turns away to*
>   *her next-door neighbour.*
>
>   OLIVER *and* BUTTERWORTH *are eyeing the food, the*
>   *plates full of leftovers.*

BUTTERWORTH: I'm hungry . . . (*He moves off with* OLIVER,
approaching a table of guests.) Excuse me. Is this
finished . . . ? And my friend . . . ? Thank you very
much, very nice, thank you . . . We're not proud . . .
we can scoop around . . . !
>   BUTTERWORTH *and* OLIVER *eat the leftovers and then*
>   *move off towards another table.* PAUL *is watching the faces*

around the tables from the past, studying how the guests
from the big house have changed. All the people he used to
know.

A voice calls out from the shadows 'Paul . . . ?'
LIZZIE *is standing in the shadows in her white dress.*

PAUL: Lizzie . . .

LIZZIE: Paul, please . . . !

PAUL: Please?

LIZZIE: Don't make trouble . . .

PAUL: Why should I make trouble . . . ? I am very happy
for you. (*He indicates* MR ZACK *and* MARCUS.) All your
other ex-bosses are here . . . (*He smiles.*) and it's good
to have a ghost at a wedding . . .

LIZZIE (*very anxious, intense*): My parents are here . . . that's
them over there. (*She indicates a working-class-looking*
couple sitting at the high table.) I want it to be special
for them –
Her new boss, ANDERS, *is suddenly re-entering the*
marquee with his heavy portable phone.

ANDERS (*to* LIZZIE): I'm sorry . . . just had to pop out
to make a quick phone call . . . having to lug this
around –

PAUL: Lizzie and you are going to work together, I gather.
ANDERS *looks puzzled at* PAUL, *feeling he has seen his*
face somewhere.

ANDERS: That's correct.

PAUL: It's a great hippo.

ANDERS: Excuse me?

PAUL: A.E.T . . . a great hippo, a big heavy company,
awkward, loads of divisions, waddling slowly. But is a
great thing to be, a hippo – very difficult to destroy . . .
ANDERS *looks at* PAUL *as if he is out of his mind.*

ANDERS: Quite. Never heard it put like that before.
LIZZIE *is desperate to move* PAUL *away from her new boss.*

LIZZIE (*hastily*): Paul likes animals . . . Paul and I used to work together . . . He was my mentor . . .

ANDERS *nods at* PAUL *and moves into the marquee.*

 LIZZIE *turns urgently to* PAUL. *She whispers to him in the shadows outside the marquee, trying not to be seen by any of the guests.*

LIZZIE: I'm sorry . . . I am . . . that I borrowed ideas for the decorations from the old days, although I did help with them too back then! . . . But I know how it must appear to you . . . I'm sorry I didn't invite you, I wasn't brave enough, I didn't know what you would do . . . (*She stares at him imploringly.*) But please, please don't ruin my wedding . . . Not in front of my parents . . . my new boss . . . *Please, Paul.*

PAUL: You really think I would . . . ?

LIZZIE: I don't know . . . you're capable of anything, Paul . . . Why are you here?

PAUL: I was curious. I knew you'd invite everybody . . . I wanted to see what they'd look like now – (*He smiles.*) I'm here because of them, really. And I wanted to wish you well, of course. I mean it, Lizzie.

LIZZIE: Thanks. You've done that OK . . . Now – *please* . . . *She suddenly almost screams. She realises the whole scene is visible on the huge video screen, because they have strayed in front of the video camera. People are staring from inside the marquee at the giant image of her on the screen as she entreats* PAUL. *People craning their necks to get a better look.*

 LIZZIE *whirls round for a second, in a panic trying to see where to go, to get away from the screen. She runs into the shadows.*

LIZZIE: JESUS! . . . (*She goes further into the shadows.*) Jesus – this is a nightmare! This is horrible . . . (*Passionately.*) Paul please . . . I'm begging you, I would kneel! – If I could in this dress . . . *please* go . . .

SNEATH *is tapping the microphone.*

SNEATH: We must have the bride back now . . . back here, Lizzie . . . The great ordeal of the speeches beckons . . .

LIZZIE: Please, Paul . . . Don't ruin things . . . maybe you think I deserve that – maybe I do – but PLEASE . . . !

PAUL: Sure. (*Calmly.*) Whatever you say. Don't want to cause any problems. I just have a notion I want to put to you sometime . . . A business proposition . . .

LIZZIE (*seizing on this*): Absolutely . . . I will call you . . . !

PAUL: You'll call me?

LIZZIE: I will. I promise. I'll call as soon as we get back from the honeymoon. I want to hear what you have to say. If you go now, I *promise* I will call you, Paul. (*She stares straight at him.*) I absolutely promise . . .

We cut to PAUL, OLIVER *and* BUTTERWORTH *walking along the pontoon bridge, in single file, back the way they came. The lighted marquee is behind them. We fade to black.*

INT. PASSAGES. THE OFFICES OF A.E.T. DAY

A long marble passage, cold but impressive, lit by heavy old lamps which are swaying very slightly in the draught. A secretary is walking towards us, her heels ringing out unnaturally loudly on the uncarpeted floor. There is an atmosphere of crisp, old-fashioned formality.

We cut to the secretary, DIANA, *knocking on a wood-panelled door and entering.* LIZZIE *is sitting behind a big desk, we see her across the expanse of a very large office. She is surrounded by more wood panelling, and solid old furnishings including the heavy lamps.*

LIZZIE *looks older, but smart and in control. The perfectly poised businesswoman sitting behind her desk.*

DIANA: Your 12.30 is here.

LIZZIE: Good. Show him straight in, Diana.

As DIANA *withdraws,* LIZZIE *moves a couple of things on
her desk. As she does so there is an explosion of loud
drilling just the other side of her office wall. She flinches
slightly at the noise, as she readies herself for her visitor.*

SNEATH *enters. He is wearing a neck-brace. He looks
more portly, the age we saw him at the beginning of the
story. He exudes affluence, and seems as confidently beady
as ever.*

LIZZIE: William, what have you done to yourself . . . ?!

SNEATH: I don't know . . . I was just in bed – (*He grins.*)
Merely sleeping, I hasten to say! . . . I must have
rolled over and fallen somehow! It's age, I think . . .
can't even turn over in bed! (*He sits nonchalantly.*) Are
we having lunch here or out?
The drill explodes again.

LIZZIE: Certainly not here, not with this happening!
They're redoing all the offices . . . We're almost the
last one like this. It'll soon be gone –
SNEATH *surveys the beautiful old office.*

SNEATH: What a pity . . . (*He grins.*) It suits this mighty
organisation – especially those lamps . . . !

LIZZIE (*warmly*): Your book is a great success, isn't it!

SNEATH (*brightening*): So you've heard? . . . It's just easy-
to-read history really – why we won the war! . . . I'm
doing Beaverbrook next, I think. Press tycoons usually
play well at the box office – and I'm going to do a
book of political gossip too, The Blob said he would
feed me a lot of useful things . . . ! (*He stares at her.*)
You look beautiful Lizzie . . . both beautiful and
amazingly in charge.
LIZZIE *smiles.*

SNEATH: The best combination there could be . . .
The drill erupts again, making the desk shake. SNEATH*'s
tone changes.*

Talking of gossip, have you ever been in touch with

Paul? . . . Since – I can't hear you – since the wedding
. . . (SNEATH *has to shout above the noise.*) Paul?! Have
you ever been in touch? . . . *Did you ever call him?*

LIZZIE: No. I keep meaning to pick up the phone.

SNEATH: As the years go by . . . it must get more difficult –

LIZZIE *looks up.*

LIZZIE: I *will* do it. One day.

We cut to SNEATH *and* LIZZIE *moving along the marble
passage, passing a door that opens into one of the big
central offices. Through the door they can see the
devastation being wreaked on this room. Through the
clouds of dust they can glimpse pieces of panelling being
ripped away and modern fittings just beginning to take
their place round the edge.*

SNEATH: A new look . . . I suppose we must all succumb
eventually –

LIZZIE*'s face suddenly clouds. Through the dust, right at
the other side of the room there is a group of young people
in dark clothes.* LIZZIE *catches a glimpse of floppy blond
hair. It is* SIMONE, *the girl who pitched the flaky food at
the venture capitalists.*

LIZZIE: I have just seen a ghost.

SNEATH (*staring through the dust*): They look unmistakably
like management consultants to me . . . Usual thing
isn't it, everyone made to reapply for their jobs. The
office makeover and then call in the consultants . . . !
(*He peers at them.*) More young people sent along to fuck
up our lives . . . (*Lightly.*) I must discover once and for
all who gave them permission to start doing that . . . !

LIZZIE *watches the group with a sense of foreboding, as
they move, shadowy figures seen through the dust.*

*The camera begins to track towards the consultants,
right into the dust cloud as the noise reaches a crescendo.
We then dissolve to the same room but with a totally
different interior.*

INT. MAIN OFFICE. A.E.T. NIGHT
There are now two glowing glass meeting rooms in the middle of the large office and modern furnishings all around. There seems to be no daylight. The blinds are drawn and we cannot be sure if it is day or night. The meeting rooms shine brightly in the surrounding muted light, like space capsules radiating brilliant white light.

We see LIZZIE *watching in the shadows. The group of now just three* MANAGEMENT CONSULTANTS *beckon towards her from inside the glass chamber.* LIZZIE *doesn't immediately respond.* SIMONE *stands on the edge of the glass meeting room.*

SIMONE: We are ready for you, Ms Thomas.

> LIZZIE *enters the glass meeting room. There are two young men in dark suits and* SIMONE. SIMONE *has an austere expression, pale skin, almost as if she is a member of a religious sect.* LIZZIE *greets her.*

LIZZIE: Hello . . . we've met before – I don't know if you remember –

SIMONE (*looking up*): I do remember . . . (*But with no smile.*) That was in another life.

INT. ANDERS' OFFICE. NIGHT
We cut to ANDERS *surrounded by a group of conspiratorial-looking executives. They are studying discussion papers spread over the table, a sense of deep concentration. The lighting is low and modern, little wall-lights sprinkling light round the room. But the room is dwarfed by the heavy lamps that still hang from the ceiling, which are now switched off. They are shifting in the draught, creaking in a slightly sinister fashion.* ANDERS *suddenly looks up at them angrily.*

ANDERS: I should never have agreed to let those lights stay . . . Keep the original fittings, they're charming,

they said . . . Well I hate them! Must get them
removed immediately!
The other executives look up at the lights.

INT. GLASS MEETING ROOM. NIGHT
We cut back to LIZZIE *in the glass meeting room. In the
shadowy outer office, people are glancing up from their work to
watch her being interrogated by the three young people.*

YOUNG MALE CONSULTANT: So I think we have covered
the ground we needed to cover . . . and Simone and I
are grateful for your co-operation and for the time
you let us sit in on your work. It has all made sense.
LIZZIE *allows herself a small smile. She does not want to
show them a lack of respect.*
LIZZIE: It all made sense? That's good . . .
SIMONE (*flicking back her floppy hair casually*): There is
just one other matter . . . We've noticed, checking on
your CV – some time ago you talked to the press
immediately after having left the employment of a Mr
Paul Reynolds. (*Sharp.*) Would you like to comment
on that?
LIZZIE *is immediately on her guard. As she hesitates, the*
MALE CONSULTANT *holds up the old press cutting:*
'Secretary Tells of Property Millionaire's Drug Den'.
Lizzie stares back at him.
LIZZIE: I shouldn't have done that. Talked to the press . . .
There was no confidentiality clause in my contract
then, but even so, I should never have done that.
SIMONE *looks up with an enquiring look.* LIZZIE *meets
her gaze.*
LIZZIE: You have to understand it was a different age . . .
It was like the end of something really, rather –

(*We move in on* LIZZIE *as she hesitates about which word of condemnation to use.*) reprehensible. It was a very indulgent and self-destructive environment I was working in. It was – well, it was almost like Hollywood really, you know, like some movie director shutting himself away on his great estate with his adoring acolytes . . . just frittering everything away, because he has had such success – he thinks he's some kind of god . . . (*We are really close on* LIZZIE *now.*) It was the last dregs of that seventies-style anarchy . . . (*She looks at them.*) I don't know if that's an excuse for what I did . . . But –

We stay on LIZZIE. *We see a sudden cut, a subjective shot going down one of the leafy paths leading to the walled garden full of exotic flowers on* PAUL*'s estate. We cut back to* LIZZIE *in the present.*

LIZZIE: But that's what it was.

INT. MAIN OFFICE / LIZZIE'S OFFICE. DAY

We cut to the rain pouring down. The blinds have been pulled up in the main office and we can see the rain bucketing down the big windows. People are sitting at their desks looking very vulnerable, fearful, watching the passage to see if they are about to be summoned.

We cut to LIZZIE *in her office, the rain patterns playing on her face. We realise immediately this is the same shot as when we first saw* LIZZIE *at the beginning of the story in her austere office. She's on the phone. We hear* SNEATH*'s voice.*

SNEATH: Did you hear me, Lizzie – *Paul is here*?! And I don't know what he wants . . . !

We see, what we did not see before, LIZZIE *is watching her secretary crossing the outer office while she is on the phone.*

*The secretary is walking towards her in an ominous fashion,
as if about to deliver some very bad news.*

LIZZIE: No, I haven't talked to Paul, I told you . . . ! I have
no idea what he wants –

We inter-cut for one brief moment to SNEATH *on the
landing of the mansion flat and a shot of* PAUL *staring
through the glass.*

*We cut back to the secretary, a dark figure standing in
the door of* LIZZIE's *office, like a messenger of doom.*

LIZZIE: I'll call you back William!

INT. ANDERS' OFFICE. DAY

LIZZIE *moves into* ANDERS' *office, trying not to look too
anxious.* ANDERS *is sitting at his desk surrounded by his tight-
knit group of executives. There is a feeling of high tension in the
room.*

ANDERS: Lizzie, please take a seat . . .

LIZZIE *sits, nobody is looking directly at her.*

ANDERS: I'm delighted to say we would very much like you
to join our team.

LIZZIE (*relieved smile*): Great . . . !

ANDERS: There are going to be some very considerable
changes and I have to warn you everything that is
discussed between us will be in the *utmost* confidence.
It can only be discussed between the individuals in
this room. And with no one else under *any*
circumstances.

LIZZIE *nods.*

ANDERS: To prepare for this, I suggest you take the rest of
the week off – while some of the people, who are less
fortunate than yourself, are leaving . . .

LIZZIE: Right. Thank you, I will. Can I ask –

ANDERS: No, no questions yet. You can try asking them,
    but I won't answer them.
    The lamps creak above their heads.
    Do something you've always meant to do in the next
    few days . . . Get as far away as possible from the
    office – and come back refreshed!
    We stay on LIZZIE's *face as she thinks about this.*

EXT. FLAT COUNTRY LANDSCAPE / INT. CAR. DAY
*We cut to a car driving along an isolated road in a very flat
landscape.* LIZZIE *is sitting in the back seat, she is very smartly
dressed. The car turns off the road and bumps along a farm
track in the middle of bleak fields. There are no buildings. We
see* LIZZIE *searching through the window for signs of any sort of
dwelling. Then we see looming on the horizon a cluster of old
farm buildings which look very decaying, almost derelict from a
distance. As they get close* LIZZIE *notices little metal structures
on some of the gate posts: small mechanical windmills spinning
in the breeze. They are models rather than practical machines.*

  We cut to LIZZIE *getting out of the car in front of the
ramshackle buildings. She indicates for the car to stay. There is
no sign of the farm inhabitants. She walks around the edge of
the buildings calling out.*

LIZZIE: Hello . . . ? Anybody home . . . ? Hello?!
    *She pushes open a metal gate that leads into the farmyard.
    She is greeted by the sight of a yard that is almost knee-
    deep in mud, with three huge pigs wallowing around the
    edge of the mud. In the middle of the yard are five small
    children aged between three and eleven. They are all
    barefoot and caked from head to foot in mud.*
ELEVEN-YEAR-OLD BOY: She's here . . . she's here! The
    lady is here!
    We see LIZZIE *in her smart clothes and shoes standing on*

the very edge of the mud staring across at the children.
Two women come out of the farm buildings; one is plump
and looks vaguely familiar. The other is in a wheelchair.
The plump woman is in her late thirties, the woman in her
wheelchair is in her late twenties. A voice calls down to
LIZZIE. *She looks up.* PAUL *is sitting in the window on the*
first floor of one of the farm buildings, his legs dangling
over the edge. He has very long hair.

PAUL: We thought you would never come.

    LIZZIE *looks across the farmyard at* PAUL *and all the*
    children.

LIZZIE: Hi! Everybody! (*She greets the women.*) Angela,
    after all these years! And Rachel too . . . ! It's amazing
    to see you! (*She looks across at the mud.*) Paul how do
    I get across? Is there any other way . . . ?

PAUL: No other way, no! Stay there Lizzie . . . don't move!
    We cut to the children scattering a path of dry straw over
    the mud. LIZZIE *is teetering along this improvised path in*
    her unsuitable clothes, trying to get across the yard.

LIZZIE (*laughs*): I might have guessed it would be an
    assault course coming to see you Paul . . . !

PAUL (*watching her progress*): You have to dress for the
    country, didn't anyone tell you –

LIZZIE: Yes . . . why do I always feel overdressed every time
    I see you . . . ?!
    She slips off the straw matting and sinks into the mud.

INT. FARM BUILDING AND HOT TUB. DAY
We cut to PAUL *and* LIZZIE *sitting inside one of the farm*
buildings staring down into a large hot tub. The tub is almost
the size of an indoor swimming pool, gentle steam is rising from
it. Several of the children are swimming about inside the tub, a
couple of them darting underwater, doing rapid turns and then
plunging up to the surface and smiling at LIZZIE. PAUL *has*

rolled himself an enormous joint and as we cut into the scene,
he is lighting up. LIZZIE *is staring at the children.*

LIZZIE: I had no idea you had a family . . . !

PAUL (*lightly*): As you see, I never do things by halves –

LIZZIE: It's such a surprise . . . ! I never thought, I never
 ever pictured you as a family man. (*She pauses.*) Are
 they . . . ? (*She hesitates.*) Are they – ?

PAUL (*grins*): From both women?

LIZZIE: Yes . . . ?

PAUL (*mischievously*): I believe so . . . (*He smiles at* LIZZIE,
 drawing on the joint.) Yes. They are. Of course.

LIZZIE: You and your harem . . . Every man's fantasy . . . !
 (*Suddenly.*) Aren't you going to ask me if I've got
 kids?

 PAUL *offers her the joint.* LIZZIE *takes it, deciding to have*
 a puff.

PAUL: You haven't, have you?

LIZZIE: You knew just by looking at me?! (*Staring at the*
 kids.) Got another Eden here have you? Far away
 from everything . . . (*Suddenly, laughing.*) You do know
 there's been an election? – After all these years Labour
 has got in – or are you *completely* out of touch . . . ?!

PAUL (*self-mocking grin*): I *think* I heard that . . .

 ANGELA *and* RACHEL *appear,* ANGELA *wheeling* RACHEL
 in her wheelchair. RACHEL *starts to undress and so does*
 ANGELA. ANGELA *helps* RACHEL *with her skirt.*

RACHEL: It's our turn, kids . . . ! Make way . . . ! It better
 be warm enough.

ANGELA: We're coming in! Make way! Anybody in our way
 gets flattened!

PAUL: You don't want to get flattened!

 ANGELA *jumps into the water naked and then gently eases*
 in RACHEL, *who is also naked.* RACHEL *turns towards*
 LIZZIE, *who is staring down at them.*

RACHEL: Never thought you'd see me here too! Never thought I'd last the distance . . . !

ANGELA: We spend a lot of our time in here . . . (*She laughs.*) A lot of the kids were conceived in this room!

PAUL takes back the huge joint. LIZZIE *is watching the naked women splash around. They have a sensual uninhibited warmth.*

PAUL: Why have you come now, Lizzie? After all this time?

LIZZIE: You invited William remember? He was too terrified to come . . . so I thought I would come instead.

PAUL: You busy?

LIZZIE: Yes. About to be fantastically busy.

PAUL (*suddenly looking straight at her*): Don't let them kill the big beast, remember . . . your company . . . Its spread is what makes it great . . . !

The ELEVEN-YEAR-OLD BOY *who is sitting on the other side of the pool suddenly calls out.*

ELEVEN-YEAR-OLD BOY: Who is the lady?

PAUL: This lady? This lady here? . . . She is my sister.

LIZZIE (*very startled*): No, no! why did you say that . . . ?

RACHEL (*calling enthusiastically*): Come on in, Lizzie . . . !

ANGELA: Come on, Lizzie . . . It's great in here! You've got to come in!

LIZZIE tries to smile but she looks ill at ease. She has no wish to join PAUL*'s harem. Both women continue to call out to her good-naturedly.*

PAUL (*grins*): Not sure we're ready for that yet . . . !

INT. PAUL'S DOMAIN. FARM BUILDING. DAY

We cut to LIZZIE *and* PAUL *inside* PAUL*'s work area, which adjoins the bathing area. Through the door* LIZZIE *can see the women having their bath,* ANGELA *now floating gently in the middle of the pool,* RACHEL *smoking a joint as she lies in the warm water.*

Inside PAUL's *workroom there is an extraordinary amount of clutter, just like when* LIZZIE *first saw his inner sanctum in the big house. There are drawings all over the walls, exquisite drawings of visionary structures. There is also a series of sketches and cartoons of characters that were his guests in the old days. Inside the room there are also computers and a keyboard; straw and rustic farmyard equipment mingles with the more high-tech stuff.*

LIZZIE: Gone back to the clutter you so love . . .

PAUL: That's right. Until I find somebody to whip it all into shape again . . . Or of course when *you* come back . . .

   LIZZIE *smiles uneasily at this.*

   LIZZIE *looks back at the women in the water.* RACHEL, *her head tilted back, calling out loudly to the children.* PAUL *follows her look.*

PAUL: Thinking just because she's disabled, doesn't mean she should have to share a lover . . . ?

   LIZZIE *turns.*

LIZZIE: I wasn't. You don't always know my thoughts. I was thinking she looked happy. (*She sees all the drawings of the past on the wall.*) Jesus, here we all are! Redfern at the picnic . . . Coyle – The Blob . . . Oliver with his sparkler . . .

PAUL: I like The Blob, whatever happens, whether he is in or out of power, he always stays the same shape – the same texture, completely round and smooth.

   LIZZIE *stares at* PAUL's *drawings of her, her different look through the years, getting smarter and more fashionable. One picture shows her peering at the crocodile.*

LIZZIE: You always keep the past with you – wherever you are . . . I've noticed that. (*She turns.*) What happened to the crocodile?

PAUL: He lives in Norway now. In luxury.

LIZZIE *is staring back at the hot tub watching the women and children.*

LIZZIE: You never told me why you were so interested in the crocodile – why it was eighth on the list?

PAUL (*inhaling on the huge joint*): It's simple. Big, big asteroid hits the Earth – end of all dinosaurs! But wait a minute – there's a huge reptile that survives totally unchanged, survives the huge bang, just the same now as two hundred million years ago! How did he manage it? The most successful form of life there has ever been? Find that out – (*He grins.*) and you could have found the secret of life . . .

LIZZIE *stares at* PAUL *disappearing in a haze of smoke and dope.*

LIZZIE: And how are you going to find it out just by keeping him in a tank?

PAUL: By thinking about it. How else?! . . . (*He indicates the view out of the window across the flat landscape.*) Using dreamtime . . . remember? (*He indicates the drawing of* REDFERN *at the picnic, standing before* PAUL *on the table.*) Kind of important, isn't it! Do *you* have time to think, Lizzie?

LIZZIE: Of course I do.

PAUL (*indicates the view*): Here's the place for thinking. (*Invitingly.*) You should give it a try sometime . . . (*Looking straight at her.*) It might have extraordinary results –

LIZZIE: Stop trying to wind me up, Paul . . . you always have an amazing knack of making me feel uncomfortable – (LIZZIE *suddenly makes out she has felt her pager go off. She takes it out of her pocket and looks at it.*) I've got a message to call work . . . I may need to go back to London early –

PAUL *gives her a sharp glance, showing he does not believe her.*

PAUL: Right. Of course. That would be a pity . . . (*He smiles.*) You don't *have* to go in the hot tub, you know. Would you stay . . . if you didn't have to go into the tub?

LIZZIE (*sharp*): I just need to go back to London, OK! (*Slowly, as if to a child.*) This is work . . . great changes are happening . . .

PAUL *smiles languidly at this.* LIZZIE *moves to the door.*

LIZZIE: Why did you say I was your sister?

PAUL (*smiles*): Aren't we brother and sister, Lizzie? (*Then gently.*) I always thought that's what we were . . .

LIZZIE: I don't know what that means . . . ! If you mean we were always fighting – yeah, we certainly did that . . . we managed that OK!

PAUL (*very laid-back smile*): Why are you getting angry, Lizzie . . . ? No need to get uptight . . .

LIZZIE *stares at him in his haze of dope.*

LIZZIE: You know I never really saw you as a hippy, Paul. I never ever imagined you'd settle for that. It's such an easy option . . . !

PAUL *blows smoke, infuriatingly relaxed.*

PAUL: Don't worry, you don't have to say I'll call you this time . . . you really don't. If you want to – just say . . . I'll see you in another six years!

LIZZIE *stares at* PAUL *with his long hair in this extraordinarily cluttered room.*

    Fade to black.

EXT./INT. OLD STYLE FACTORY. DAY

A fast steadicam shot moving with LIZZIE *as she crosses the courtyard in front of an old factory. A big industrial building. We can hear the sound of heavy machines. She goes through the main entrance to find* ANDERS *and the other executives standing waiting for her impatiently.*

ANDERS: Ah! There you are!

LIZZIE: I'm not late, am I?! I hope I'm not late?

ANDERS: Exactly on time! We will do this tour very quickly
... It is obvious why we are here and it will get even
more obvious –

*We see the executives moving through the factory, the
landscape of old manufacturing. The factory is making
vacuum cleaners and they stand everywhere, like sentries
from another age. The executives brush past them, as if
their very existence offends them. They pass through the
canteen where all the dinner ladies are lined up beaming a
welcome, with huge trays of currant buns displayed for
them.* ANDERS *and his team are not stopping. They pass
members of the workforce, who are lining to greet them,
with barely a nod. They go through a room plastered with
old-style pin-ups, snorting derision at the décor. All this in
a series of ruthless fast cuts.*

Suddenly ANDERS *stops the executives in an area where
they find themselves alone with all the vacuum cleaners
lined up in a series of rows facing them.* ANDERS *banishes
the management team of the factory who have been
showing them around.*

ANDERS: I need a moment alone with my team, thank you.
(*He turns to the executives.*) I have to say this now –
because it is all the more powerful while we are in
amongst it. This is the past, everybody! This is *over*!
We will be ridding ourselves of all these factories – we
make everything from these vacuum cleaners to lamp
posts, from soap to helicopters – it's ridiculous! It will
all be shed. The terrible load we've been carrying is
going to be off our backs at last ... ! (*Triumphantly he
turns to the rows of vacuum cleaners and addresses them
directly.*) It's gone ... we're rid of you all! (*He moves
in the sea of vacuum cleaners.*) It's been due for years
and now finally we can DO IT! (*He turns surrounded*

*by all the vacuum cleaners and beams at his executives
and* LIZZIE.) Not a word of this of course! Not yet . . .
not a single word!
We cut to ANDERS, *the executives and* LIZZIE *going back
into the canteen. All the tea ladies start to move towards
them with their offerings, the groaning trays of food which
themselves seem out of date.*

LIZZIE (*whispers to one of the executives, as she watches all the
employees*): Who's going to tell them? And when?

INT. LIZZIE'S OFFICE. EVENING
LIZZIE *is looking down a list contained in a confidential folder
as her secretary is tidying. A TV is playing silently in the
corner, a cartoon is on the screen.*

LIZZIE (*whispers to herself in surprise*): Jesus! . . . we're
buying all this?!
DIANA, *her secretary, looks up.*
LIZZIE: Sorry, I am talking to myself . . .
DIANA *switches the TV off.*
LIZZIE: No, leave it on . . .
DIANA *looks disapproving.*
LIZZIE: When I first started I always had a TV playing
silently, helps me concentrate . . . (*She stares at the
list.*)
DIANA *switches the cartoon back on.*

INT. ANDERS' OFFICE. DAY
We cut to the executives, ANDERS *and* LIZZIE *sitting round a
new table, an interesting shaped table with a hole in the middle.
The heavy lights are still there. The executives are studying two
pieces of paper each.*

ANDERS: Everything on this list is *going* . . . everything on this other list is a potential purchase . . . (*He glances up at the old lights with a cheerful chuckle.*) And at last we've got a replacement for those . . . (*Directly at the lights.*) They managed to survive for a year longer than I wanted – but the end is in sight now! (*Then he faces the executives.*) We will be buying every internet and every telecom company we can lay our hands on. We have a huge cash cow and now we are going to milk it, well and truly! The share price will be sixteen pounds or seventeen within a year . . . There will be the most dramatic growth in the company's history . . . maybe in any company's history . . . !

The executives' faces tense, excited.

LIZZIE: It's amazing what we are buying . . . but are we going to spread the risk? If they're all internet and telecom companies . . . if things were to slow –

ANDERS: Telecom is an energy force unlike any other . . . it cannot slow! (*The lights creak.* ANDERS *views them with a gleeful look.*)

INT. LIZZIE'S OFFICE. NIGHT

LIZZIE *is working late on her computer, and studying pages of statistics. It is night. The TV is playing silently. She looks up suddenly.* PAUL *is sitting in a chair which is in a slightly surreal position in the middle of the outer office. He is rolling a cigarette. He looks straight at* LIZZIE.

PAUL: You know of course this plan is bollocks . . .

LIZZIE *looks around with a start. There is no one there, just a darkened office.*

She is seeing things. She immediately decides to go home.

We cut to her walking along the passage with her coat on. There is a strange noise coming from the end of the passage. A weird crashing noise. She moves through the door from where the noise is coming to find ANDERS *and two men in overalls standing by an open window. There is a pile of the old lamps lying in a great dead heap in the middle of the room.* ANDERS *and the men are lobbing the lamps one by one down into a skip a hundred feet below. They are watching them smash on impact and celebrating each time they do so.* ANDERS *is tossing them down with an almost manic expression on his face. He sees* LIZZIE *and grins.*

ANDERS: Why does this give me such pleasure, Lizzie? Because we were being so slow . . . so very slow to take action . . . to get this company to join the real world!

We see LIZZIE *stare down at the old lamps smashing into the skip like exploding flour bombs. They continue to fall, forming vivid patterns of scattering white glass. We fade to black.*

INT. LIZZIE'S OFFICE. SUMMER EVENING

We cut to LIZZIE *working at her desk. It is a stifling summer evening. The air conditioning is going full blast, there are pieces of paper fluttering like ribbons all round the office. There are fans on too.* LIZZIE *is sweating as she works. The television is playing silently in the corner.* LIZZIE *has her head turned away from it as she works. We see behind her on the TV screen the image of crocodiles. And people in white coats in laboratories, then more crocodiles and then test tubes full of blood, and then more crocodiles.*

LIZZIE *suddenly looks up as if she senses something. She sees the images, for a second she doesn't concentrate on them and*

*then something makes her scramble on the desk trying to find
the remote and get the volume on. She turns on the sound just
in time to hear: 'These crocodiles live in the filthiest water in the
world. They constantly fight and receive severe wounds but these
never become infected. They possess one of the most powerful
antibiotics in their system known to science. If this antibiotic
could be harnessed . . . or could be copied . . . '*

LIZZIE *stares at the screen for a moment in wonderment. She
picks up the phone and dials rapidly. The phone rings and
rings.*

LIZZIE: Be there, Paul . . . Be there!
    *We see a quick cut of the deserted farm buildings with the
    phone ringing and ringing unanswered.*

INT. ANDERS' OFFICE. NIGHT
We cut to ANDERS *and the executives sitting at the table with
the hole in the middle. A high shot seen through the new
modern lights that glow above their heads.* ANDERS *is giving a
report to his fellow executives.* LIZZIE *is sitting directly opposite
him.*

ANDERS: Studying these results, I want to issue a health
    warning – just looking at them, it will seem some of
    our acquisitions are not performing, that there has
    been a slow-down in the telecom sector, but this is
    because we are in a process of transition . . . in the
    middle of the cycle . . . Things are not what they
    seem.
    As he has been saying this we are moving in on LIZZIE.
    *We are very close, her eyes filling the screen. Suddenly we
    cut to* PAUL *standing in front of the dinner ladies and
    some of the workforce in the canteen of the vacuum cleaner*

factory. PAUL *is surrounded by a line of vacuum cleaners
and is addressing the staff in an exuberant manner.*

PAUL: The only thing these need is a little tweak – (*He twirls
a vacuum cleaner round.*) a little redesign, a little poke
and a prod and we are set for the twenty-first century.
People will always need to clean their homes . . . ! We
have a future!

*The dinner ladies beam and applaud. The image melts to
the now empty factory, machinery idle, water dripping in.
The sound of applause dying away as we see the dead
factory.*

　We cut to LIZZIE*'s eyes and then we see* PAUL *suddenly
in the middle of the glass meeting room, swinging round on
his chair.*

PAUL: Gentlemen, this bowl is a Fear Bowl . . . people in
years to come will look at this in bewilderment,
because it is a power bowl, a terror bowl, a bowl
guaranteed to make people more stupid . . .

We are back on LIZZIE*'s eyes. Then we are moving down
a passage near her office.* PAUL *is standing in a window
with two vacuum cleaners either side of him. He looks
back at her.*

PAUL: Why did you agree to this, Lizzie . . . ?

We cut back to LIZZIE. ANDERS*' voice is calling 'Lizzie,
Lizzie are you with us?'* LIZZIE *suddenly looks at all her
fellow executives, their fleshy confident faces.*

LIZZIE: Have we thought enough about what we are
doing?

ANDERS (*startled*): Thought enough?!

LIZZIE: We are pouring money away. We have sold off
seventy-five of our businesses, sometimes giving them
only a day's notice of what's happening to them . . .
We are now thinking of making another twenty or
thirty thousand people redundant . . . The share price

is in free fall. So yes, I'm just wondering, have we been doing enough thinking, gentlemen?!

ANDERS (*icily*): We *all* committed to this strategy – there's no turning back. *Naturally.* No possibility for second thoughts. Now, no word about these job losses must leak out, of course. Remember, the results are not what they seem.

EXT. FLAT COUNTRY LANDSCAPE. DAY

We cut to a line of tractors crossing the horizon. PAUL *is driving the first,* ANGELA *the second, a farm-hand the third. In the carts behind the tractors are the children and* RACHEL *and heaps of belongings.*

INT. LIZZIE'S OFFICE. DAY

We cut to LIZZIE *sitting in a totally empty office. The whole floor of offices is empty. There is a hushed atmosphere. She is looking very pale and sitting very straight.*

DIANA *appears in the doorway across the office.* LIZZIE *does not look up.*

LIZZIE: It's the time for the meeting. I do realise.

DIANA: Yes . . . (*She's regarding* LIZZIE *with a cold stare.*) You know I just heard on the radio . . . the share price has gone under a pound . . . (*Her voice rising in disbelief.*) It's now just 75p! How could that happen?

LIZZIE (*mechanically*): I know . . . but not everything is what it seems. (*We move very close to* LIZZIE*'s face, her voice hushed.*) Twenty thousand people losing their jobs . . . but it's not what it seems . . .

We fade to white.

INT. FOYER/CONFERENCE ROOM. SHAREHOLDERS'
MEETING. DAY

We dissolve from the sharp white light to SNEATH *moving from
the foyer of A.E.T headquarters, into the edge of the
shareholders' meeting. He is right at the back. The colour is
bleached out, all the faces looking pale, stunned, disbelieving.*
SNEATH *has to crane his neck to get a view. Right in the
distance on the platform is* ANDERS, *three other male executives
and* LIZZIE. *We cut to* ANDERS, *he is in full flight trying to cast
as bland a spell as possible on the meeting.*

ANDERS: I can only repeat, once the full business cycle is
    played out, we will be in a much stronger position
    than we ever were before.

WOMAN: When will the whole cycle have taken place?

ANDERS: Well, it is difficult to be precise. (*His voice begins
    to fade out and continues under the stirrings of
    discontent.*) These results cannot be taken in isolation.
    The strategy is only in its first phase, and nobody
    could – or did – foresee the slowdown in telecoms,
    which has slightly altered the speed of the process . . .
    altered but in no way derailed it . . .
    *We continue to hear his voice rambling on in the
    background. We are with* SNEATH *at his position at the
    back of the hall.* SNEATH *is glancing around at all the
    listening faces, which are taut with tension and anger.
    There among the shareholders are* REDFERN, COYLE, *the*
    ALBERT BROTHERS, MARCUS *and* MR ZACK. *They all
    look shaken, totally shocked.* SNEATH *moves to get close to
    them.*

REDFERN: It's amazing what they've done! Completely
    incredible . . . One of the biggest companies in Europe
    has been destroyed in just under two years . . . !

COYLE: It is a train wreck . . . staggering in its ineptitude . . .
    inexplicable stupidity . . . arrogance on a quite epic

scale . . . ! How could clever people be so stupid?!
Many people will be ruined . . . their life savings . . .
SNEATH *looks at the faces all around.*

SNEATH: When you look at people as they are losing
money, they literally seem to change colour, don't
they . . . ? I've lost thousand and thousands – (*Slight
grin.*) and I've certainly changed colour . . .
*We see people in the audience beginning to shake with
apprehension and mounting anger.*

Suddenly ANDERS *has stood up.*

ANDERS: And now I think you will all understand, because
of the sensitivity of the present situation there is a
limit to what I can say at this juncture . . . and there
is a lot of business to do, and I have in fact a very
important meeting to attend right now – in no sense a
crisis meeting – which I must travel to without further
delay . . .
ANDERS *leaves the podium. Somebody screams at him
from the shareholders: 'Going to negotiate your big payoff
are you, you bastard?'*

The other executives hastily follow ANDERS *off the
podium, as people shout and yell at them, demanding
answers to their questions. Only* LIZZIE *remains, a lone
figure on the platform, facing a room packed with enraged
shareholders. The mood of anger is growing rapidly
amongst the audience. They are losing their inhibitions
about where they are. People are crying out . . . 'Your
strategy has cost me everything!' . . . 'You can't just walk
away!' . . . 'I have lost all my life savings' . . . etc.*

LIZZIE *stares down at them. She is ashen.*

LIZZIE: There will be a full statement in due course.
I promise you . . . about the present situation . . .
Nobody is trying to evade or run away from anything.
Out of the corner of her eye she can see ANDERS *and the
other executives scuttling away down the backstage*

*passage. The crowd catch a glimpse of this. They suddenly
start to lurch forward. People are beside themselves with
fury, yelling and shouting.*

*LIZZIE gets up and leaves, as boos rain down after her.
The uproar continues, people swirling, trying to follow her.*

*As LIZZIE crosses out of the conference room, she sees all
the waiting media gathered in the foyer waiting for news
from the shareholders' meeting. There are TV camera
crews, press photographers and reporters. LIZZIE stares at
them for a moment, at the predatory cluster.*

SECURITY MAN: This way, Ms Thomas, must take you to
the car.

LIZZIE: No, just give me a moment . . .

*And then she decides to face them. She turns and moves
towards them. LIZZIE looks incredibly isolated, as she
moves slowly across the shiny floor of the foyer. We see this
small figure approach the barrage of cameras and
photographers. LIZZIE blinks in the sharp white light.
Shareholders are beginning to spill out of the conference
hall and are pushing forward to get a look at LIZZIE from
behind the waiting media. There is a sudden crush, people
angrily demanding to be able to see and hear what she has
to say. There are also people staring down from the upper
galleries. Suddenly there seem to be people swarming
everywhere. For a moment LIZZIE turns, slowly taking
this all in, as people heckle her from above. She then
stands in front of the waiting media, staring straight at
them, trying very hard not to let her voice shake.*

LIZZIE: I'm here, ladies and gentlemen . . . to tell you we
fully intend to face up to what has happened, and
explain it with the utmost clarity. We were – we are –
the custodians of a great company. A very great
company. And if there have been mistakes, I for one
will not shirk my responsibility . . . nor seek to avoid
the blame . . .

FEMALE REPORTER: Lizzie, what about all the people who have lost money?

MALE REPORTER: What about the twenty thousand people who lost their jobs?

LIZZIE: I have nothing further to add.

The flash photography is blindingly bright. LIZZIE *is engulfed by reporters surging all around her, as she mouths again and again: 'I have nothing further to add'.*

INT. LIZZIE AND RALPH'S HOUSE. DAY

We cut to LIZZIE *in the foreground of the shot vomiting into the sink of her bathroom, her whole body convulsing. She continues to shake and shiver after she has finished being sick.*

We then dissolve to her lying curled up in a ball, completely white, and shaking like a frightened animal as her whole house is surrounded by the press pack. They are at the window, they are baying and banging on the doors. The phone is ringing and ringing. Her husband RALPH *is yelling at them to back off. The noise surrounding the house is deafening.*

We dissolve and find LIZZIE *sitting on the stairs in the falling light. She is in a T-shirt and jeans and barefoot, and has retreated deep in the shadows.* RALPH *is at the front door: it is chained but is open a crack, and he is talking through this opening. He is telling the waiting media that she will under no circumstances be making any further statements. In the foreground of the shot the phone is ringing and ringing.*

We move in on LIZZIE. *She is shivering and shaking, there is still a frightening noise all around the house. We see on the television the image of her on the news walking slowly across the foyer to face the press, blinking as all their flashes go off. The image is playing silently. We keep moving in on* LIZZIE *as she lies in the shadows.*

A sudden cut. We're moving along the paths in the big house. The light is brilliantly bright and vivid. We see the sculptures,

*the statues, the little silver tents sprinkled all over the grounds.
We see images we have never seen before, of* OLIVER *as a boy
joyfully holding forth in the garden,* PAUL *moving among the
exotic flowers. The* ALBERT BROTHERS' *sculpture of a giant
butterfly floating like a huge kite over the garden. The garden is
a place full of rich possibilities, the colours are so intense.*

And all the time we see PAUL, *moving in his domain. The
camera travels fast through the gate of the walled garden to
discover a landscape inside the garden far richer than we had
ever seen before. It is as if we are remembering it differently. In
the middle of it* PAUL *is sitting confidently, surrounded by all
his papers.*

RALPH's *voice is calling 'Lizzie, Lizzie it's Paul . . . !'*

We cut back out of the flashback, as LIZZIE *turns sharply,
staring towards the phone.*

Time cut. LIZZIE *is sitting on the bottom step of the stairs,
tears are pouring down her cheeks. But she is full of anger and
frustration rather than self-pity.*

LIZZIE (*into the phone*): You're going . . . you're going to
    say I TOLD YOU SO . . . ! And I can't bear that . . .
    I *can't bear* to hear that, Paul!
    We intercut with PAUL *in a tiled old schoolroom. He
    is leaning against an old-fashioned wooden school desk.
    We intercut between him and* LIZZIE.

PAUL: Would I say that?

LIZZIE: Yes, you fucking would . . . ! Of course you would.
    I can't believe . . . I can't believe what I've done . . .
    I could see it all happening, the amazing stupidity of
    it all – and I couldn't do anything, I couldn't STOP
    IT! You once said I destroy everything I touch . . .

PAUL: *You* haven't destroyed anything.

LIZZIE: I was party to it, I agreed, I sat there . . . I was
    with them! I saw all those people lose their jobs . . .
    and when everything was going wrong I couldn't find

you, you bastard, I couldn't get in touch. Even when I saw about the crocodiles . . . (*Tears are pouring down her cheeks but she is trying to stop them coming, flicking them away.*)

PAUL: I have moved, that's why you couldn't find me . . . I have left the farm. You were right – being a hippy was too easy . . .

LIZZIE: I hear you're making money again! Your chain of bookshops is doing OK. So you can watch all this feeling really good. Because you got it right, didn't you?! Jesus, Paul – I don't want to have to think of you every day for the rest of my life saying 'I got it right, didn't I, Lizzie!' –

PAUL (*slight smile*): Well, I can think of worse punishments.

LIZZIE (*laughing despite herself, but the tears are still rolling down her cheeks*): What is this Paul . . . ? You and me . . . ? I just don't understand – I love my husband . . . He is sitting watching me now – talking to a man he doesn't know . . . talking like this . . . And I love him . . . I REALLY LOVE HIM . . . And I don't love you, not in that way, I have *never* loved you in *that* way –

PAUL (*simply*): I know –

LIZZIE: Why is it then that I think about you so much . . . ? Why is it that often you are the first thing I think about in the morning? When I wake . . . you know, what would Paul say about this . . . ? About what I am about to do . . . ? What would Paul feel about that? . . . It's crazy . . . ! I didn't even know you'd had a family and yet I think about you all the time . . . What is that called, Paul?! . . . Going bonkers, probably! Why is that happening . . . ?

PAUL: Because we were born to work together but we couldn't manage it. And we can't stop thinking about it.

LIZZIE: And that was MY FAULT, I suppose?!

PAUL (*calmly*): Absolutely not. People need to work with other people that threaten them, that challenge them, but they will never ever *let* themselves work with such people . . . It was me who didn't let that happen . . . (*Softly.*) You stayed as long as you could . . .

Pause. We stay on LIZZIE's *face for a moment.*

LIZZIE: Why is it whenever I think of that bloody garden . . .

We see the past, camera travelling though the garden, the vivid colours.

. . . it seems so magical? . . . So *special* . . . ? And it hurts that we didn't do more . . . it really hurts me . . . Sometimes I think we could have done so much!

PAUL *is trying to reply but she goes on:*

And yet – no listen to this – and yet it was *hell* at the time . . . that was the reality . . . it was HELL. wasn't it?!

PAUL (*lightly*): There were hellish moments . . . and not such hellish moments . . . It depends what you like to remember.

LIZZIE: What is all this tactful stuff?! This diplomatic bollocks . . . ! I'm curled up here in a ball, thinking my life is over . . . and you're giving me all this bland shit! You should tell me what you really think . . .

PAUL: You know what I really think, Lizzie. We should work together . . . I've thought that for ages . . .

LIZZIE: Why? It's only always been a disaster! Anyway, you don't think I've got a creative bone in my body – you never have! You just want me to tidy up after you, colour-code the papers . . .

PAUL (*calm smile*): That's certainly not true. You are one of the most creative people I know –

LIZZIE: I like 'one of the most'! (*Then, more softly.*) You've never said that to me before . . .

PAUL: I should have –

LIZZIE: Don't start all that brother and sister stuff again
    please . . . if you do that I'm hanging up. I just feel
    so foolish, Paul . . . so incredibly foolish. So many 'if
    only's . . . so many fucking 'if only's . . .

PAUL: I've moved into an old school, had you heard that?
    I'm doing it up. And I'm having a party.

    LIZZIE *can't help smiling at this.*

PAUL: I think you should come . . .

EXT. THE PLAYGROUND OF AN OLD VICTORIAN SCHOOL.
NIGHT

*We cut to the grounds and playground of an old Victorian
school on the edge of the city. We crane in on the scene. A high
shot of a big bonfire and the surrounding landscape. All the
characters are there,* COYLE, SNEATH, REDFERN, *the* ALBERT
BROTHERS, *and* BUTTERWORTH. *They are all looking pale
and old in contrast to* RACHEL, ANGELA, OLIVER *and the
small children, who are full of exhilaration which is infectious,
and which begins to spread among the chubby white men.*

Amongst them all, PAUL *is moving gracefully, his hair cut:
he looks rejuvenated. He looks younger than he has done for
years, smartly dressed but yet another different look.*

OLIVER *is spurring the others on, to bring things out of the
old schoolhouse and to throw them on the bonfire. The
characters are lugging out old desks, bits of old wood, old doors,
all sorts of rubbish and furniture.* OLIVER *seems full of a new
energy, his depression lifted.*

OLIVER: We've got to burn all this and more! (*As he lugs
    wood.*) Anybody want to ask me a question while we
    are doing this? Any question you like . . . ! I'll get it!

REDFERN: Ah! OK, what was the first ever vessel to go
    through the Panama Canal?

OLIVER: That's too difficult! Even for me! But I'll tell you the day of the week they opened the Panama Canal – it was a Tuesday!

LIZZIE *is in a party dress, looking more relaxed, if still pale. She is with her husband,* RALPH. *She sees* RACHEL *and* ANGELA *together, their obvious shared love for* PAUL, *their faces glowing with the light of the fire. She sees* PAUL's *children playing with the sparklers. She sees* SNEATH, *beady as ever, trying to do as little carrying as possible. She sees the* ALBERT BROTHERS, *portly businessmen now throwing things into the fire with some of their old energy and life. She sees* BUTTERWORTH *sitting quite close to the bonfire, eating boiled sweets and not helping at all.*

PAUL *comes up to* LIZZIE. *They sit together on a low wall, watching the characters and the fire.* LIZZIE *is holding a sparkler.*

LIZZIE: You got them all doing some *work* for a change . . . (*She laughs.*) I was thinking you gave most of them a start in their careers – and then I came along and lost them all their money . . .

PAUL (*grins*): I don't think I'll argue with that . . .

LIZZIE: Or I could say we *both* blew it . . . ! The boss and the secretary . . . (*She turns and looks at him and then back at the sparkler.*) I want to ask you one question and only one and don't answer too quick . . . promise?

PAUL *nods.*

LIZZIE: All those years ago . . . could it have been different? What happened? I mean our work together?

PAUL: No.

LIZZIE: That was much too quick! You didn't even think about it!

PAUL: No. I don't have to . . . because we do best on the phone. But now with e-mail we could set up a business and we need never ever be in the same room . . . in fact we need never ever *see* each other if we don't

want! Just think Lizzie . . . we'd be unstoppable –
(*Looks straight at her.*) *Now* we'd be unbeatable . . .

LIZZIE (*laughs*): You're incorrigible, Paul.

PAUL: Is that – go on, tell me more? I'm intrigued?

*LIZZIE is staring into the fire. She then looks up at PAUL.
Her tone is warm, positive.*

LIZZIE: It might be . . .

*The moment is held as we see both PAUL and LIZZIE
thinking about the real possibility of working together
again.*

*Then we see all the characters' faces round the bonfire,
watching the old furniture from the school burn. They stare
at the flames for a long moment. We start to track back
away from them all, they are beginning to disappear from
us. Then we hear BUTTERWORTH's voice piping up.*

BUTTERWORTH: Don't tell anyone yet, but you will be
thrilled to hear my writing is nearly finished – I'm on
the last page of my book!

*We are now far away from them as they move round the
bonfire.*

We fade to black.

GIDEON'S DAUGHTER

Gideon's Daughter was produced by Talkback Productions Ltd for BBC Television and was first screened in February 2006 by BBC1. The cast was as follows:

Gideon	Bill Nighy
Stella	Miranda Richardson
Natasha	Emily Blunt
Sneath	Robert Lindsay
Barbara	Ronni Ancona
Andrew	Tom Hardy
Dent	Tom Goodman-Hill
Diane	Joanna Page
Bill	David Westhead
Becca	Samantha Whittaker
Badalamenti	Kerry Shale
Badalamenti's Spokesman	Daniel Mendoza
Petersen	Cate Fowler
American Producer	Michael Fitzpatrick
Hospital Stranger	Graham Cull
Compère	Julia Malewski
Comic	Jason Manford
Miller	Bobby Bragg
Young Natasha	Rebecca Bridges
Sneath's Son	Leonard Dalrymple
Girl playing Richard III	Jennifer Higham
Gideon's Wife	Natasha Alexander
Gideon's Father	David Annen
Teenage Gideon	Shane Allan
Young Gideon	Baily Scougall-McCurry

Director Stephen Poliakoff
Producer Nicolas Brown
Line Producer Helen Flint
Music Adrian Johnston
Director of Photography Barry Ackroyd BSC
Editor Clare Douglas
Production Designer James Merifield

CREDIT SEQUENCE

The camera is moving along a road, an ordinary street, the lens floating very close to the surface, just a few inches above it. We sail past bollards and then slip across a zebra-crossing, the black and white stripes seeming very abstract because we are so close.

Then the camera discovers a garland of flowers lying in the middle of the road, on the white lines. The camera travels past the garland and along the white lines until it hits another bunch of flowers, and then another and then another, until the camera reaches a road hump. It floats over the road hump slowly like scaling a mountain and stares down on the other side at the rest of the street.

The whole road is full of flowers for as far as the eye can see, strewn over the tarmac but packed tightly together. Bright exotic colours turning the drab street into something tropical and intense.

There is a loud rapid knocking on the soundtrack.

INT. SNEATH'S FLAT. DAY

We are in SNEATH's *cluttered apartment. An old-style mansion flat, full of books, periodicals and some interesting modern pictures.* SNEATH, *a ruffled man of indeterminate age, is plodding towards the knocking. His face can look comparatively youthful and full of vitality, but when his mood changes suddenly it becomes tormented and older.*

At this precise moment he is wearing only his pyjama bottoms, and looks alarming.

As he pads through his flat, the credit sequence finishes.

SNEATH *shouts at the door as the knocking continues.*

SNEATH: I'm coming . . . I'm coming!

> *He pulls open the door.* BECCA, *a young girl of twenty-one, is standing in the passage. She is dressed for the office and is holding a laptop. She is very pretty, with a fresh, eager expression.*

SNEATH: You're from the agency? (*He stares at her big eyes.*) Jesus, you're young . . . ! Come on in –

BECCA *hesitates, seeing* SNEATH*'s naked chest and his loose striped pyjama bottoms, the pyjama cord dangling half undone.*

SNEATH: What're you waiting for? Come on in, for goodness' sake . . . I'm just getting everything ready –

He is moving back inside the flat where the heavy curtains are still drawn. SNEATH *pulls the corner of a curtain back, so a shaft of sunlight plunges into the room. His manner is breezy but businesslike.*

SNEATH: No time to waste, not at the rate you charge! . . . And knowing how slow I am . . . (*He tugs at his pyjamas and stares at* BECCA *in the pool of sunlight.*) You're very lovely . . . !

BECCA *stares back at him, nervous, completely uncertain what to make of him.*

BECCA: Are we starting right away?

SNEATH: Yes, if that's not too much to ask! (*He looks puzzled at her nervousness, then stares at his bare feet, ignoring his floppy pyjama bottoms.*) Is it my feet that are worrying you? They are cleaner than they look . . . As we get on with it, I'll put on more clothes . . .

BECCA *starts setting up her laptop as* SNEATH *continues. She keeps glancing over her shoulder, watching him.*

SNEATH: Except I haven't quite decided which one to do first . . .

He stops again as BECCA *glances over her shoulder.*

You're so very young, so exquisite, I will have to do most of this standing with my back to you . . . stop myself getting distracted . . . (*Suddenly his voice much more intense.*) I lie . . . *Who am I kidding*?!

BECCA (*startled*): Excuse me . . . ?

SNEATH *is suddenly pacing, striding the room in his pyjama bottoms.*

SNEATH: I said I lie . . . I know perfectly well I have to do the one I can't get out of my head . . . (*He stares straight at* BECCA.) A little scary, a little extraordinary . . . my favourite story . . . (*He stops pacing.*) The Millennium . . .

BECCA looks at him, her big eyes wide with puzzlement. SNEATH grins.

SNEATH: You too young to remember the Millennium?!

BECCA (*nervously*): Which Millennium?

SNEATH: Which Millennium?!! You've been alive for two of them have you ?! . . . Which Millennium – Jesus . . . ! *The Millennium!* The most important night supposedly for a thousand years.

BECCA: Right . . . of course I know *that* Millennium . . . I got confused –

SNEATH: The night when nation showed off to nation . . . ! Remember now . . . ?

We see an image of the Queen on Millennium night lighting a hideous metal beacon with 'British Gas' emblazoned all over it.

SNEATH's voice continues over the image.

SNEATH: The river of fire . . . the ghastly beacon . . . the Dome . . . all of that! Did the earth move for you . . . ? *We cut back to* SNEATH. BECCA *is watching him apprehensively.*

SNEATH: Heartbreakingly empty wasn't it . . . ? Full of people of course . . . but so utterly empty! *Then his face falls. Suddenly a haunted look as if a memory has pierced him to the heart.* BECCA *looks concerned.*

BECCA: Should I start now, Mr Sneath? Should I be typing this?

SNEATH: Any second . . . (*He snaps out of the sombre mood and smiles.*) It's like one of those awful quizzes on the radio . . . when you want to throw the set into the

bath . . . ! 'What links the French novelist Georges
Simenon, said to have slept with over two thousand
women, cycle lanes, and the Queen of England
lighting her disgusting beacon on Millennium night?'
*We see the image of the beacon again with the British Gas
logo dwarfing the Queen as she lights it. The flame leaps up.
The image increases in size and graininess all the time. We
cut back to* SNEATH *who is pulling at his pyjama trousers.*

SNEATH: The curious link between those furious French
buttocks and the Queen . . .

BECCA*'s anxious young face staring at* SNEATH. *She is
beginning to think she should leave.*

SNEATH: No, no, don't look like that! It's OK, I'm just
writing a book . . . You're safe here I promise . . . I'm
going to pace though, be prepared for that! (*He paces,
his pyjama cord flopping; he glances down.*) And I'll
make sure there's no X-certificate glimpses from
down there, or failing that – they're kept to the
absolute minimum . . .

He stops in the middle of the room.

Start, let's start with the red carpet . . .

*The camera is already skimming along the red carpet,
initially a few inches above the surface as* SNEATH*'s voice
continues.*

That should get us both going . . .

EXT. / INT. APPROACH TO A WEST END CINEMA AND
FOYER. EARLY EVENING

We are moving with SNEATH *along the edge of the red carpet
outside a West End cinema. There is absolutely torrential rain
pouring relentlessly down on the awaiting throng. It is a film
première and there are paparazzi lined up all along the carpet.
The general public are roped off at a safe distance, watching the
arriving guests.*

The soap begins to appear on the red carpet at the movie première

Gideon and Andrew stare down at the banquet after the movie première

Gideon approaches Stella during the re-enactment of her son's last bicycle ride

Bill dragging Petersen, the council leader, along the street

Natasha sings her unexpected song at the school assembly

Gideon meets Bill in the park as he collects some of Princess Diana's flowers

Stella in her bedroom with Gideon: 'Don't worry, I'm not going to leap on you'

Gideon and Stella near the isolated church

Sneath, Becca and Frederick together in the park at the end of the story

Natasha finds Gideon unable to move backstage at the comedy club

Natasha in the fifties ball gown the week she leaves home

We hear SNEATH*'s voice-over as we watch him weaving his way among the photographers and the guests. He is in evening dress and trying very hard not to get soaked.*

SNEATH (*voice-over*): It is May 1997, barely a couple of weeks after the end of eighteen years of Tory rule, Labour's colossal first victory.

    A film première, nothing very special, a big action movie – I try to get myself invited to as many premières as I can. You never know who you're going to meet. As it turned out, the exploding carpet was by far the best feature of the evening . . .

We see people picking their way along the red carpet, heading towards the cinema. The guests cannot drive right up to the entrance, they have to walk the length of the carpet to get in. There are plenty of flunkies scurrying around with umbrellas trying to protect the valuable hair and frocks of the famous. But all the guests are forced to pick their way very gingerly along the carpet. Because of the torrential rain, the carpet has begun to misbehave. The weight of water has released the traces of detergent used to clean the carpet and it is bubbling up, beginning to froth and turn into a white foam.

    We see the expensively clad feet trying to negotiate the unsightly white puddles along the carpet.

    SNEATH *ducks into the foyer and then turns to watch the spectacle with a beady look of satisfaction. Suddenly he sees standing in the shadows a tall, handsome man in his forties, watching, with an amused expression, the celebrities battling their way towards the lighted foyer.*

    A young girl of eighteen is standing next to him in a shimmering evening dress.

SNEATH: Gideon . . . *you're* here! Terrific. The evening goes up a couple of notches already!

GIDEON (*charming smile*): Shameless flattery as always, Will . . .

SNEATH: But it's true! You can't deny it!

GIDEON (*indicating the young girl*): Do you know my
daughter, Natasha?

SNEATH: Natasha?! Good Lord – what a beautiful young
woman you are now . . . ! Last time I met you, you
were in the bath, playing with a huge blue sponge,
a tiny speck of a girl –

NATASHA *smiles, determined not to show embarrassment.*

NATASHA: But of course. I remember it well . . .

*The celebrities are sloshing along the carpet as the white
foam is increasing in severity. Some of them are slipping
badly, much to the delight of the watching photographers.
The fans are calling out encouragement, as the guests
slither their way to safety. They are shapes in the rain
trying to keep their dignity.*

*In the foyer there are many flunkies with towels and
buckets trying discreetly to wipe the carpet, fighting the
flood and the foam. It is a completely one-sided battle as
the rain pours down mercilessly.* SNEATH *watches in delight.*

SNEATH: Isn't it fantastic?! I love it. And what's even
better – the invitations all had to go out before the
election . . . so there are plenty from the old regime
here trying to put a brave face on it . . . ! (*He waves
merrily at an old Tory.*) I might write a quick book
about them!

SNEATH's *eyes are darting around the foyer. We see that as
well as the soaked glamorous young things there are plenty
of stout politicians and anonymous looking transatlantic
executives. Everybody is wet. Some still have white foam
on their shoes.*

GIDEON (*lightly*): I need to find some stars, Will, to say
hello to us . . . to impress this young lady. (*Indicating*
NATASHA.) Otherwise she will say I've got her here
under false pretences –

SNEATH: No need to worry about that . . . ! (*He turns to*

NATASHA.) They'll make a beeline for your dad, just
you watch . . .

Indeed we see people glancing respectfully in GIDEON's
direction, nods and smiles, people wanting to catch his eye.

*The carpet is now a river, the procession of guests
acutely conscious of the surrealism of their approach to
the cinema, the fact that their celebrity walk through the
photographers has been reduced to a shambles. They are
now dodging and diving along the carpet.*

Suddenly a young starlet, DIANE, *takes her shoes off
and walks defiantly barefoot and without an umbrella the
full length of the carpet, dangling her shoes ostentatiously
in her hand. She is applauded all the way by the fans, as
the flash photography explodes.*

DIANE *appears totally drenched in the foyer brushing
aside the offer of towels from the flunkies. She sees* GIDEON
*in the shadows and immediately approaches him, ignoring
everybody else who is coming up to her or trying to catch
her eye.*

NATASHA: Oh my God . . .

GIDEON: This is how to do it.

NATASHA: She looks amazing!

DIANE: Gideon . . . ! Wonderful to see you! (*She kisses
him.*)

GIDEON: That was some entrance, Diane . . .

DIANE: You bet! I'm not one to look a gift horse in the
teeth – (*She laughs merrily.*) or whatever the expression
is . . . So glad you're here Gideon! If I could *wish*
somebody to be here – anybody in the world – you're
the one!

GIDEON (*amused grin, correcting her*): One of the ones. Just
possibly . . . !

DIANE (*lightly*): One of the ones! If you insist –

*People are brushing past them, sneaking respectful glances
at* DIANE *and* GIDEON *together.*

GIDEON: My daughter Natasha, you haven't met –

DIANE: Your daughter?! What a gorgeous daughter you have, Gideon . . . (*She impulsively gives* NATASHA *a kiss.*) You *are* gorgeous Natasha! (*Then softly:*) You were so right about *that* book Gideon, and I was so thick to think it could have ever made a movie – Dullsville times twenty! You were so much righter than my agent . . . I fired him, no I did, the lazy creep. (*Her tone urgent and intimate as the photographers begin to crowd round her.*) I want to talk to you so much, Gideon . . . I mean, I know you don't do personal PR any more, far too grand –

GIDEON: Yes, I do . . . (*A teasing smile.*) A few people . . .

DIANE: You do! Great . . . The chosen ones! The lucky few. How do I become one of those? I'll commit murder to become one of them.

GIDEON (*charming smile*): You just pick up the phone.

DIANE: Liar! That definitely isn't true. That's such a lie . . . ! (*Then the urgent tone again.*) I have to ask your advice, Gideon . . .

The flash photography is going on ceaselessly as the photographers crowd round DIANE, *but she is oblivious. She whispers to* GIDEON:

Something very small and something else rather huge . . .

People are calling out to DIANE.

DIANE: I'll try calling you very early one day. I know that is the only time to get you Gideon, really really early.

She is moving off, surrounded by people.

Isn't this lovely? It's like being on the *Titanic* . . . !

INT. HOTEL BALLROOM. NIGHT

We cut to the meal after the movie, a gala of round tables in a modern hotel ballroom. We see sharp cuts of the faces at the different tables, the young starlets, the fleshy old Tory politicians, the excited younger faces of the new regime.

GIDEON *is sitting eating at a table where he has a fine view of the whole room.* NATASHA *is sitting next to him and there is an empty chair on the other side.* GIDEON *has a very minimalist helping of food – he is hardly eating, watching the room with amused detachment. All around him the noise of chattering voices is absolutely deafening.* SNEATH *is sitting at a nearby table; he calls across at* GIDEON. GIDEON *mouths back that he can't hear.* SNEATH *leaps up and comes across, still chomping a mouthful of food. He puts both fingers in his ears, indicating the level of noise.*

SNEATH: I'm gobbling, as usual . . . and you're eating like a bird as always.

GIDEON (*smiles*): I stuff myself at home, of course . . .

SNEATH (*to* NATASHA): I have to discuss this with your dad – the seating plan, it's always fascinating . . . and tonight even more than usual!

We see the different tables and the flushed faces.

The old Tories still near the centre of the room, but definitely already been edged outwards – next time they'll be right by the kitchens.

We see the fleshy disappointed faces.

They can't believe they've said goodbye to power . . . Some of those old codgers will be sidling up to you, Gideon, in a minute to see if you can help them make a bob or two . . . .

GIDEON *smiles.*

GIDEON: Table 6 is interesting . . .

We see a sharp-faced young man whose leg is twitching with adrenaline; he is rocking in his chair almost as if he has got an affliction. We suddenly see, through GIDEON's *eyes, how fidgety all these powerful people are: bread rolls are being crumbled without being eaten, napkins are dabbing mouths too frequently, hair is being flicked.*

SNEATH (*to* NATASHA): And all the time . . . just watch –
　　people are glancing up at your dad . . . See there –
　　He indicates eyes flicking towards them, checking them out.

GIDEON (*grins*): Stop hyping me to my own daughter,
　　Will, for Chrissake!

　　NATASHA *watching people stealing glances towards her father.*

SNEATH (*lightly, leaning close to* NATASHA): He doesn't like
　　the truth, your dad . . . but don't be fooled by this
　　modesty . . . (*He smiles.*) He doesn't need to work the
　　room, for instance, because he has got someone else
　　doing it for him.

　　We see a young man, ANDREW, *moving round the room,
　　chatting and flirting from table to table. He is a febrile,
　　animated figure. He glances up very briefly to catch*
　　GIDEON*'s eye before he moves on to another table. We feel
　　a connection between the two men, a current running
　　between them.* GIDEON *sits surveying the room, very still
　　and stylish, while* ANDREW *works the tables energetically.*

NATASHA: I've met Andrew . . . (*Watching him across the
　　room.*) He's always like that – never still for a single
　　moment!

SNEATH: That's how your dad can afford to sit like this,
　　lord of all he surveys.

　　A handsome, dark-haired woman, BARBARA, *appears and
　　slips into the empty chair next to* GIDEON. *She is very
　　fashionably dressed; there is a sharp professional sheen to
　　her. She is younger than* GIDEON.

BARBARA: Hi, darling . . . (*She kisses him and sits.*) Thought
　　I would skip the movie, it's usually safe to do that –
　　very loud was it? . . . (*Without waiting for an answer.*)
　　If anybody asks I can say it was wonderfully loud,
　　can't I?! Hi, Natasha! (*She turns to* SNEATH.) Will,
　　you're always at these things aren't you, every single
　　one I have ever been to!

SNEATH: I try my best.

BARBARA: It's buzzing in here anyway, it hit me even out
there in the passage . . . I'm going to enjoy tonight –
ANDREW *catches* GIDEON*'s eye, makes a very discreet
signal, but* SNEATH *notices.*

SNEATH: Ah! A signal – a signal that cannot be ignored . . . !

GIDEON (*getting up*): Excuse me.

INT. HOTEL LAVATORY. NIGHT

A large art deco gentlemen's lavatory. ANDREW *and* GIDEON
*are standing either end of a line of handsome washbasins. The
lavatory is momentarily deserted.* ANDREW *is full of energy, but
he has an infectious laugh which gives his vitality warmth as
well as danger.*

ANDREW: Amazing vibe in that room, isn't there?!

GIDEON: You too? That's what Barbara said . . .

ANDREW: You must be able to feel it?! They are all so
excited to be in power . . . (*He grins.*) It's very ripply
in there – it's great!

GIDEON: So what's so urgent Andrew?

ANDREW *turns from the basins, grinning delightedly.*

ANDREW: A messenger is coming! (*Slowly.*) We are going
to receive an important message!

GIDEON: When?

ANDREW: Tomorrow morning, Nicholas Dent wants to
come and see us tomorrow –

GIDEON: Nick Dent! (*Incredulous.*) He's an important
messenger?! I don't believe it . . .

ANDREW (*unfazed*): Why not? He's just outside the
cabinet . . . The first reshuffle he'll be in – (*Breezily.*)
Anyway, he's got a tremendously important message
for us –

GIDEON: I can't fit him in tomorrow.

ANDREW: He's willing to come very early, as early as you
like . . . !

ANDREW *turns nonchalantly to examine the little round*
soaps that are in coloured paper by each basin, like Easter
eggs, as he waits for GIDEON*'s reaction.*

ANDREW: These little soaps are nice, each one a different
smell! (*He picks up an example of each one.*) Apricot . . .
orange . . . honeysuckle . . . (*He grins broadly, boyishly.*)
It's a night for stealing soap, isn't it!
He puts the cluster of soaps in his dinner-jacket pocket and
tosses one to GIDEON. GIDEON *catches the soap.*

GIDEON: And what *is* his message?

ANDREW: Something so big . . . so momentous, we can't
even begin to guess. If we try it'd be hopeless, we
won't even get close!

GIDEON: That probably means he wants advice on how to
restyle his hair . . .

ANDREW: No. He knows you don't do that any more. It'll
change all our lives he said . . .

GIDEON (*dry smile*): Do we want our lives changed?
ANDREW *grins.*

ANDREW: Maybe! . . . Who knows?!
A little American man with large glasses enters the lavatory.
ANDREW *greets him shamelessly, without missing a beat.*

ANDREW: *Great* movie, Steve! Noisy certainly, but the
chases, the tunnels, all that was really well done. And
the splat – great splat-factor! It'll be a monster hit . . .
The AMERICAN PRODUCER *grunts and moves over to the*
urinals. GIDEON *watches him carefully.*

GIDEON: I liked the ducks . . .

AMERICAN PRODUCER (*as he pees*): You know . . . the
ducks are my favourite bit.

INT. PASSAGE/HOTEL BALLROOM. NIGHT
A passage leading to the ballroom. We can see the throng through
the door, eating, gossiping – the noise is deafening. Outside the

rain is still pouring down relentlessly. ANDREW *and* GIDEON
are moving back to the ballroom; some guests acknowledge
GIDEON *as they pass.* GIDEON *and* ANDREW *pause in the*
doorway, surveying all the tables. GIDEON *indicates* ANDREW's
jacket pocket, bulging with soap.

GIDEON: You smell extraordinary.

ANDREW: Good. Hopefully it'll confuse everybody who
comes up to me! (*As they stare into the ballroom.*) She
looks great, your daughter.

NATASHA *shimmering in her dress.*

ANDREW: A chip off the old block . . .

GIDEON *is staring across at the ballroom, at his daughter*
glowing in her dress and BARBARA *and all the chattering*
faces. For a moment and quite abruptly the sound of the
chatter cuts out, we stay on GIDEON's *eyes, and then look*
back at all the faces. The swirl of excited people.

ANDREW's *face suddenly appears in front of* GIDEON,
very close to the camera.

ANDREW: Gideon?! . . . HELLO . . . !

The sound cuts back sharply, all the hubbub returns.
Shall I tell him to come? In the morning? . . . The
messenger? . . . How about 6.45?

GIDEON (*as if he's been listening all the time*): No . . . ten
past seven.

He stares back at the ballroom. ANDREW, *at his shoulder,*
grins.

ANDREW: It's going to be a busy time for us, Gideon . . .

INT. HALLWAY OF GIDEON'S OFFICE BUILDING. EARLY
MORNING

We cut to the elegant eighteenth-century hallway of a large
London house. DENT *and his young male assistant are sitting*
on two wooden chairs in the lobby, looking like patients waiting
for the dentist. The early morning sun is just beginning to

illuminate the interior. DENT *is a thin tall man of about forty, he has an expansive bantering manner and a very loud laugh.*

DENT: What time is it?

AIDE: Seven-sixteen.

DENT (*laughs*): He keeps *me* waiting . . . ! The bastard . . . !

> *A young woman appears above them on the fine eighteenth-century staircase. The two men fall silent; they can't stop themselves behaving as if they are somewhere very formal.*

YOUNG WOMAN: Mr Dent? Gideon is ready for you now.

INT. FIRST FLOOR OF GIDEON'S OFFICE. EARLY MORNING

We cut to the young woman escorting DENT *through the outer office. We see* GIDEON's *outfit is housed in two eighteenth-century houses that have been knocked together. Large Georgian windows let the light flood in. On all the walls are huge framed photographs, very striking images, unusual glimpses of children, of technology, of urban landscapes. The whole atmosphere is simultaneously grand and soothing. Fresh fruit and juice are displayed on the table – deep colours, plum juice, apricot juice. The young staff are already at their desks, working away.*

DENT (*grinning as he passes the photographs*): Great pictures! Do you do copies? Must get copies of one or two of these . . . !

> *At the end of the open-plan office, they can see* GIDEON *waiting in a fine elegant room, sitting behind a very big desk.* ANDREW *is hovering in the doorway.*

DENT (*calling across*): Jesus . . . Gideon! It's like coming to visit some European ambassador! (*He reaches the door of the office.*) Or some incredibly expensive shrink. (*He looks around.*) Can one get any grander than this . . . ?

GIDEON (*self-deprecating smile*): It's good, isn't it? (*He swings his chair very slightly towards the window.*) I like this view particularly . . . (*He indicates the view across the garden square.*) I have to sit with my back to it – (*He smiles.*) otherwise I'd never listen to a word anybody said . . .

As he says this he glances down into the street. An old lady is walking two tiny little dogs. He is about to look away when a couple walking along the street appear just in his peripheral vision, a bulky middle-aged man and a woman in her forties. They are bustling along the pavement very fast, in a slightly strange way. He catches a momentary glimpse of them.

He turns back. DENT *is still standing in the doorway.*

GIDEON (*grins*): Sit, Nick . . . please . . . ! Can I offer you anything? Juice, we've got plum juice, or . . .

DENT *flings himself into a chair opposite.*

DENT (*lightly*): I'll skip all refreshments, not going to waste any valuable time with you negotiating my coffee order!

GIDEON: No plum juice . . . ?

DENT *suddenly points at the large photograph that dominates* GIDEON's *office. It is a splendid image of a Lancashire Bomber dropping a great column of poppies on a crowd outside Buckingham Palace on the anniversary of VJ Day.*

Next to the big colour picture are a series of black-and-white images of normal streets with flowers falling in them from the sky like snowflakes, a child crouching on the pavement with petals in his hair, a woman pushing a supermarket trolley through a cloud of descending poppies.

DENT: That was a fantastic idea, Gideon . . . ! Was it VE Day or VJ Day anniversary? That plane and those flowers . . . it said it all!

ANDREW (*cheerily*): That was his masterpiece, yes . . . what made it great, though, was not the bit outside Buckingham Palace . . . but continuing it afterwards.

The plane flew on – dropping flowers all the time . . .
leaving this trail right across the city – (*Indicates the*
pictures.) over supermarkets, over housing estates, bus
stations, school playgrounds . . . and all the time
mixing the flowers, too . . . poppies and large white
daisies . . . I love the daisies!

As he is saying this we see for a moment a quick cut of
live action, a continuation of one of the black-and-white
still images. The child on the pavement crouching,
whooping delightedly, as a snowstorm of white daisies falls
all around him.

We cut back to GIDEON, *watching both* DENT *and*
ANDREW *closely.*

GIDEON: Blimey, you two! . . . What am I being softened
up for? . . . I see you've already briefed Andrew! (*He*
looks at DENT.) What is this momentous thing?

DENT: Something that is perfect for you.

GIDEON: Which is?

DENT: We're probably going to go ahead with this Dome,
you know this wonderful magic Tory Dome that is
going to rise by the Thames –

GIDEON: It'll cost you a billion, that Dome . . .

DENT: No, no, the cost is nothing like that . . . ! (*Laughs.*)
Not remotely! Of course we would love your input
towards the Dome – (*He smiles.*) and we will expect
it – but what we've got for you is even bigger! The
Dome only makes sense of course if we sell Britain
itself to the world, every city, every bit of shoreline . . .
The Thames! We want you to place the Dome in the
wider canvas . . . the jewel inside the much bigger
jewel, make this country number one in the world on
the night in question, the most important night for a
thousand years. Now you can't get bigger than that,
can you Gideon?!

GIDEON *is watching the strange couple disappearing at
a rapid rate along the pavement below the window.*

GIDEON: So church bells ringing out . . . illuminated
Morris dancers round the bonfire . . . tightrope
walkers – in each city centre? That's what you want?

DENT: That is precisely what we don't want. (*He smiles.*)
We want to make our friends in the regions rise to the
challenge while making them think it's their idea in
the first place. (*He laughs.*) What you're brilliant at . . .
It looks like Saatchi's will do the Dome, but you're
ideal for the whole country . . . ! (*He grins.*)

ANDREW: No political baggage.

DENT: Marvellously free of baggage!
His pager goes off. He struggles with it.
We're all wired now. Jump to it like electric puppets.
So?
ANDREW *is looking excited.* GIDEON *smiles but doesn't
reply.*

DENT: After all, you've got to have something pretty
gigantic to do Gideon – to go with these ridiculous
offices!

GIDEON (*smiles and gets up*): I'll walk you out. I've got to
go to another meeting.

EXT. LONDON STREET. DAY
GIDEON *and* DENT *are walking along a busy London street
that runs in front of* GIDEON's *office.*

DENT: My car is just around the corner . . . Would you run
ahead and get it? I'll meet you at the end of the road.
He dispatches his AIDE *to run round the corner and get
the car to come nearer. The* AIDE *disappears from view.*

DENT: You become a minister and you think, great, now
my car can wait for me on double yellow lines, but

not a bit of it! Quite the contrary! (*He laughs loudly.*)
I don't qualify for a detective – I might get shot
walking to my car and then what?

At the very moment DENT *is saying this, a large burly
man literally smashes into him. He grabs* DENT*'s arm
and holds him tightly, almost like holding a lover. A woman
is standing right by him.* GIDEON *recognises them as the
couple he was watching from his window.*

The man, BILL, *is shrieking at* DENT *with extraordinary
passion, an intense ferocity. His wife,* STELLA, *is holding a
large file, full of papers.*

BILL: Mr Dent, you have broken your promise, you have
totally broken your promise . . . AND I WILL NOT
HAVE IT . . . I CAN TELL YOU I WILL NOT
STAND FOR IT ANY MORE . . . !

*DENT is looking shocked, but he obviously knows the big
burly man for he immediately starts to try to reason with
him.*

DENT: Mr Hawthorne, I have *not* broken any promises . . .
You know perfectly well I have written a number of
letters about your case and will continue to do so . . .
Now, will you let go of me?

STELLA: Bill, don't hold him like that . . . (*Trying to calm
him.*) Bill, remember what we said . . . ?

BILL (*totally oblivious of her more reasonable tone*): You *have*
broken your word, you said you would arrange what
we asked – you said you would make it happen . . .
Nothing has changed, nothing has happened . . . !
(*He is holding on really tight.*)

DENT: Mr Hawthorne, will you please let go . . . let go of
me at once . . . and I will explain.

BILL: You can't explain . . . There is no *explaining* to do.

BILL's face is huge and intense, so close to DENT*'s their
faces are almost touching.*

BILL: Two years this has been going on for, two years . . .
and we go round and round and round . . . and
nothing is *done*, nothing happens . . . !

STELLA: Bill, please let go. (*Then she turns to* DENT.) But it
is outrageous, it is completely outrageous you haven't
done anything yet –

*A coach has drawn up further along the road, full of
schoolkids. And as the scene erupts all along the street,
the schoolkids pour out of the coach onto the pavement,
staring in wonderment at these adults locked physically
together, with one of them screaming at the top of his voice.*

BILL*'s passionate assault has pulled* DENT *away from*
GIDEON *along the pavement. When* GIDEON *reaches
them he tries to intervene.*

GIDEON (*to* BILL): Let him go . . . come on . . . and then
we can see what can be done –

DENT (*ignoring* GIDEON*'s intervention*): If you come to my
next surgery –

BILL: *Surgery*?! . . . I've been to your surgery again and
again and what good does it do me?! You hide behind
each other, you just say anything, try anything, to get
rid of us, but *nothing* ever happens . . . AND I CAN
ASSURE YOU – YOU WILL NEVER GET RID OF
ME!

His passion is terrifying, really raw and from the heart.

STELLA: Bill is right – there is no point in him ever coming
to another surgery . . .

BILL: You're in power now, for heavens sake . . . ! You're
in government . . . ! And what we ask is so *small*! So
pathetically small – and easy to do . . .

GIDEON: We'll make the calls, whatever needs to happen.
I will see Mr Dent and I will make the calls . . .

STELLA: And who the hell are you?

GIDEON: Mr Dent is a client of mine. (*Indicating* DENT
and himself.) He and I will go inside now – that is my

office over there – if you let go . . . We will go in there
now and start making the calls . . .

STELLA: You don't even know what this is about . . .

BILL (*dangerous*): It's just another way of fobbing me off
and you know it is . . . It'll lead nowhere like everything
else . . .

*But he has let DENT go. GIDEON starts trying to steer
DENT back along the pavement towards his office. BILL
is following, just a few inches away.*

GIDEON: We're going in there right now . . . to start
making those calls, like I said.

BILL: Go on then . . . !

DENT (*nods*): That's correct . . . that is what we are going
to do.

*As GIDEON and DENT move off, watched by all the
fascinated schoolkids, BILL shrieks after them.*

BILL: Go on then get in there, get in there and make them
calls and you'd better understand, pal! . . . I will never
ever GIVE UP . . . !

INT. THE HALLWAY. GIDEON'S OFFICE. DAY
*We cut to GIDEON and DENT in the eighteenth-century hallway.
DENT is almost vomiting, his head bent coughing, breathing
very fast, looking at his arms to see how bruised he is.*

DENT: Are they still there . . . ?

GIDEON (*staring through the window out into the street, where
BILL and STELLA are staring back at them*): Oh yes . . .
they're still there –

DENT (*fumbling for his mobile phone*): I ought to phone the
car . . . they'll think I've vanished off the street . . .

GIDEON: What is this about?

DENT: Oh . . . it's just one of those cases . . . You've never
been to an MP's surgery have you?

GIDEON *shakes his head.*

DENT: So many nutters . . . obsessed people . . . deranged
people . . . he's one of those . . .

We see a cut of BILL *sitting in his overcoat in a passage
outside* DENT*'s surgery. He is surrounded by a huge mound
of paper, and is sorting through it methodically as he waits.*

BILL (*to a woman sitting next to him*): I've been here sixty-
eight times!

We cut back to DENT.

DENT: It's something very simple and sad. Their child was
killed, their son, on his bicycle, first time he had ever
ridden it out on the street . . . he was going down a
cycle lane . . . There's no scandal, no lawsuit possible.
They just want to show me as the local MP and all
the relevant members of the local council that they
consider the cycle lane was dangerously routed –

GIDEON: And why on earth can't they do that?

DENT: They've drawn endless diagrams . . . and we've
looked at them . . . but what they want is us all there,
standing where it happened, so he can demonstrate,
walk up and down and show us –

GIDEON: So why won't you go?!

DENT: *I'll* go . . . of course *I'll* go! But getting all the
council representatives and me there all at the same
time, such a simple thing – has proved impossible . . .
The council hate me . . . they've been advised against
taking part . . . it goes on and on . . .

GIDEON stares across at STELLA *and* BILL, *who are still
outside in the street, watching the entrance from across the
way.*

GIDEON: That's all they want?

DENT: At the moment –

GIDEON: *I'll* try to arrange it –

DENT: Why would you arrange it? Why would you want to
do that?

GIDEON: Well, we can't have you being stalked all over
London, can we?

EXT. LONDON STREET. CYCLE PATH. DAY
*A crane-shot lifting over some trees and staring down for a
moment at a strange scene. There is a road with a cycle lane
running down towards a major intersection. A group of about
forty people are at one end of the road and there is a group of
about fifteen standing at the opposite end of the road. In
between there are one or two officials and spectators dotted
along the length of the cycle lane. Far away in the distance are
police cars cordoning off the road and* DENT's *ministerial car.*

We cut to ground level just as GIDEON *reaches the scene,
standing on the periphery, watching carefully. We see everything
through his eyes.*

The large bulky shape of BILL *is standing in the middle of
the road. He is dressed in quite a smart suit, but he is wearing
trainers. He is holding a sheaf of paper and a small loudhailer.
From a distance he looks an undeniably comic figure, but as
we get close we see how truly determined he is to make his
demonstration go well. He begins to pace the route, along the
cycle track.*

DENT *is some distance away from* GIDEON *at the opposite
end of the street from the representatives of the council. He is
surrounded by his aides, who are all smartly dressed.*

*At the other end of the road are the council representatives,
a very much larger group, with their advisors and transport
consultants. In the middle of this group there is a tall very pale
woman,* PETERSEN, *the council leader, watching* BILL *with a
reluctant chilly stare. Her consultants are whispering in her ear.*

GIDEON *watches these young advisors, young men and
women in both groups. They are constantly twitching, making
notes, flicking their ballpoint pens, checking their phones,
checking their pagers – continuous edgy movement.*

DENT *stands with a fixed smile, hoping to get through the whole situation as painlessly as possible.*

Near GIDEON *on the pavement is* STELLA. *She is smartly dressed but very much in her own style: slightly eccentric, vivid clothes in surprisingly bright colours, almost as if she is at a wedding.* STELLA *is holding both a stills camera and a video camera. She follows* GIDEON's *stare towards the febrile advisors.*

STELLA: A twitchy bunch aren't they . . . !

GIDEON (*lightly*): Always, wherever you go now, there are the advisors –

There is a sudden flurry of umbrellas being unfurled in unison by all the officials.

STELLA (*laughs*): And it's only a few spots of rain . . .

GIDEON *notices a garland of fresh flowers lying next to one particular part of the cycle lane. There is also a child's bicycle up against a wall with a curl of flowers round the handlebars.* BILL *is doing up the laces of his trainers in the middle of the road. He moves over and adjusts the position of the garland of flowers a moment before he starts his demonstration.* STELLA *lifts her camera to try to photograph this gesture.*

PETERSEN (*calling the length of the street*): No photographs! We agreed *no* photographs!

Her advisors all start chorusing, 'No photographs . . . the agreement was no photographs!'

STELLA: Just thought it was worth a try!

She slings the cameras round her neck ostentatiously. The advisors see this and continue calling, 'No photographs . . . no cameras.'

STELLA (*to* GIDEON): They can't stop me wearing them!

BILL *lifts his little loudhailer which makes a rather cracked sound as he calls through it.*

BILL: Can everybody hear me? . . . (*No reaction.*) Can you hear me – yes or no?!

There are various calls from both ends of the street that they can hear him.

So we will do the first demonstration on foot . . . and then I will re-enact my son's last bicycle ride. (*He moves across to the cycle lane.*) So . . . my son – (*He stops himself.*) *Our* son, Adam . . . came round this corner here, you see . . . and he comes round, using the cycle lane, just as he is meant to do . . . (*His bulky shape treading delicately along the cycle lane.*) Keeping close to the curb . . . as you can see, his view is obscured by this overhanging tree and the curve of the wall, and most particularly by the big red pillar-box that is standing right at the edge of the cycle lane . . . There are no warnings, no bollards, no signs of any kind that the busy intersection lies ahead . . . He is cycling here – straight into the path of the oncoming traffic . . .

He has gone round the corner and is out of sight from both groups of onlookers.

He suddenly reappears, standing in the middle of the road. He calls the length of the road to PETERSEN *and the representatives of the council.*

BILL: You are too far away!

STELLA (*calling out*): They can hear you . . . it's all right, Bill –

BILL (*ignoring her*): You are too far away . . . everybody's too far away . . . !

He begins to march down the middle of the road, aiming straight for PETERSEN *and the councillors.*

BILL: The agreement was that we would walk the route . . . (*He is about to reach* PETERSEN.)

PETERSEN: We can see very well from here . . . we have an excellent view . . .

BILL: The agreement was we'd *walk* the route.

PETERSEN: There was no agreement to walk the route.

There was an agreement to attend this meeting, and
to *observe* the route . . .

BILL (*his voice rising to a menacing pitch*): No, there was an
agreement, a *formal* agreement to walk the route –
He suddenly grabs PETERSEN *by the hair. He pulls her
along the road by the roots of her hair towards the cycle lane.*

*The image goes into slow motion as soon as he has got
hold of her, this huge man pulling this pale slender woman
along the street by her hair: it is a startling image of a
man taking out his grief on someone as he pulls her along
the street.*

BILL *is surprisingly nimble on his feet, and he makes
rapid progress pulling the thrashing and incandescent*
PETERSEN.

*Behind him there is an eruption of movement, as the
advisors launch off in pursuit, their umbrellas scattering
in all directions. They eventually converge on* BILL *and
surround him, but not before he has reached the edge of
the cycle track and is forcing* PETERSEN *to stare at it,
almost as if he intends to rub her face in the road.*

They catch hold of BILL *and pull him away from*
PETERSEN. STELLA *is rushing towards* BILL *from the
other end of the street, yelling across as she does so, while
about six advisors hold onto him and restrain him.*

STELLA: Let him go . . . it'll be all right, let him *go* . . . He
won't do anything more . . . LET HIM GO!
The advisors let BILL *go, just as the police arrive to try to
take full control of the situation.*

BILL (*yells*): They broke their agreement! . . . They
completely broke our agreement –
People are surrounding him, trying to keep hold of him.
All right, I'm calm, I'm calm, thank you. I'm calm.
*He suddenly moves off, before the police can restrain him,
and gets onto the child's bicycle. He peddles furiously off
down the street away from them, and then curls round*

suddenly and unexpectedly speeds along the centre of the road heading straight back towards the group of councillors and police who are standing in his path. They scatter across the road as he approaches them really fast. He shouts at them as he sails through them.

BILL: You'll all be back . . . ! When I do it my way . . . !
He hurtles through the group and they stare after him as he disappears from view, the flowers bouncing on the handle bars.

  GIDEON *watches this huge man bicycling furiously away from them on the child's bicycle.*

  DENT *immediately gives* GIDEON *a knowing look.*

DENT: Thank God that's over . . .
DENT disappears with his entourage toward his ministerial car.

  We see from the crane-shot all the officials moving off, walking rapidly, full of relief that BILL *blew it, that he has made it so easy for them.*

  STELLA *is standing near* GIDEON.

GIDEON: I'm sorry, that's not what should have happened.
STELLA is staring after where BILL *disappeared. Her tone is surprisingly light.*

STELLA: I was sort of expecting it . . . Bill has to do these things . . . He takes out his rage on people . . . It helps him . . . I don't get embarrassed any more . . . I don't think he'll ever *really* hurt anyone. (*She suddenly grins.*) Her face?! That council leader's face, when he had her by the hair . . . it was worth coming to see that! And all those officials . . . (*She laughs.*) their faces too . . . !

GIDEON (*staring down the street*): Do you know where he was going? Do you need to catch him up? I can give you a lift . . .

STELLA: No, he's off now . . . I don't need to catch him up. (*She smiles.*) But a lift would be good . . .

INT. GIDEON'S CAR. DAY

We cut to GIDEON *driving his smart Mercedes.* STELLA *is sitting in the passenger seat fiddling with her cameras.*

STELLA (*laughs*): What a strange occasion that was . . . all those officials . . . You know, I think I got some pictures, well I *know* I got some pictures, just wonder if the one of her being dragged along will come out –

GIDEON *watching her, intrigued by her upbeat manner.*

GIDEON: Where can I drop you?

STELLA: Well, I am going all the way home to Southall, (*She smiles.*) I really don't suppose you want to take me there! . . . So the tube will be fine . . .

GIDEON *looks at her, surprised.*

STELLA: I don't live round here any more, no . . . Bill and I are not together now.

GIDEON: I'm sorry . . . Was that after the accident?

STELLA: Well, you know, things are never simple are they? It had been brewing for a while . . . (*She smiles.*) But we are friends. (*She laughs.*) Even when he is attacking people . . . (*She glances out of the window.*) I have a slightly different method of getting by . . . (*Then, conscious that* GIDEON *is glancing at her.*) So you are an advisor too, aren't you? . . . An image-maker?

GIDEON: Yes, that's right, I suppose. (*He smiles.*) A consultant . . . for a variety of things –

STELLA: For the government? And all that sort of thing? You can drop me off here, if you could –

GIDEON *draws in.*

GIDEON: Are you sure?

STELLA: Yeah, that'll be fine. So where are you going now? A bunch of VIPs, some more politicians?

GIDEON: Ah no! I'm going to my daughter's school, as it happens, it's the end-of-term assembly, her last one – she's leaving school, and she's doing a poem or something –

STELLA: That's great. Are you going to tape it?

GIDEON (*startled*): Tape it?

STELLA: Yes, video it? You've got to video it, her last
school assembly – you really must! You'll regret it if
you don't . . . You'll want to look back on it, see her
on her last day at school . . . (*Offering her video
camera.*) You can borrow this.

GIDEON: No, thank you, that's very kind, but I couldn't . . .

STELLA: Rubbish! Come on . . . (*She pushes the camera
towards him.*) You don't want to be seen videoing at
your daughter's posh school, that's it, isn't it?! (*She
laughs.*) Too embarrassed! Come on – take it!

She is getting out of the car.

GIDEON: How do I get it back to you?

STELLA: That's easy . . . (*She gives him a card through the
window.*) I work there . . . between nine o'clock at
night and seven in the morning – every weekday . . .
You can have it dropped off there –

GIDEON (*startled*): You work at night?

STELLA (*smiles*): Yes, why not?

And she is off down the street.

INT. SCHOOL ASSEMBLY HALL. DAY

We are with GIDEON *as he moves into the school hall of an
all-girls public school. It is the middle of the sixth-form
assembly, the leavers' show. Their parents are watching and
members of staff – about a hundred and eighty adults sitting in
neat rows on severe metal chairs. Several classes of the younger
girls are also sitting watching on the floor in front of the adults.
As* GIDEON *appears the assembly is in full flow, an eighteen-
year-old girl is doing a soliloquy from* Richard III, *contorting
herself into a rather over-the-top hunchback.* GIDEON *slips into
a vacant seat near the back as the girl is finishing her soliloquy.
He fiddles with the video camera self-consciously, as he sees no*

*other parent is videoing the occasion, nor any member of the
staff. There is an array of rather formidable-looking teachers
sitting in a row at the side of the hall, glancing in his direction
as he makes a slight noise.* GIDEON *holds the camera very low,
so it is level with his knees and is he hopes less visible.*

*There is polite applause for Richard III, then a thin eighteen-
year-old girl, the compère, comes on.*

COMPÈRE: And now Natasha Warner and Gabriella
    Laquaz with something they have written themselves.
    They describe it as 'a French surprise'. (*Little coy
    laugh.*) Sounds interesting to me . . . !

    NATASHA *walks on stage with* GABRIELLA, *a dark-haired
    South American-looking girl who is holding a guitar and
    stands a few paces behind* NATASHA *on stage.* NATASHA
    *sits very confidently on a high stool by the microphone.
    She is wearing a very short dress.* GIDEON *is startled to
    see this sexual, confident young woman.*

NATASHA: So . . . (*A very small cough.*) Georges Simenon
    was a French writer, a famous writer, of police stories.
    He created a great detective and slept with hundreds
    and hundreds of women . . .

    *A surprised rustle, a murmur goes through the watching
    parents.*

    Maybe . . . two *thousand* women – if we are to believe
    the man himself!

    Eyes flash in GIDEON's *direction from the stern teachers.*

NATASHA: His daughter, Marie-Jo, felt an extraordinary,
    unnaturally strong love for him, for her dad, obsessive
    love . . . and in the end she killed herself, at the age
    of twenty-five. So this is a song about that . . . (*She
    glances at* GABRIELLA *and is about to start, then stops
    herself.*) Oh the title . . . ! It's just called 'Papa' . . .

    NATASHA *launches into the song, which is in the form of a
    little folk melody, about obsessive love: very simple, quite
    tuneful. The lyrics are in English and are quite shocking*

in their intensity despite the pretty guitar melody that
accompanies them. NATASHA *sings it looking very poised*
and in command. GIDEON *is still holding the camera by*
his knees, so he only catches half of her on the image. But
we move in on his eyes; he is transfixed by the sight of his
daughter singing this love song on a very surprising
subject. At first she is not looking at him as she sings; she
is just performing it with a sharp directness and confidence.
But as the song progresses she begins to stare straight at
him, their eyes meet.

NATASHA:

> I see you from my window
> > Walking with her there
> I don't need to know which number
> > I won't stop you touch her hair.
>
> I don't need to see you waving
> > When you slip away at night
> I don't have to know what happened
> > As you crawl back when it's light.
>
> I don't need you to look at me
> > And tell how many hundreds there have been
> I don't want to have to listen
> > As they fall, a constant stream.
>
> I don't need to catch you with them
> > Your voice so full of joy
> As you murmur your little nothings
> > My own papa, so very coy.
>
> Mon cherie papa, mon cherie papa . . . .
>
> I don't need you to say you love me
> > I don't need you to say good night
> I don't need you to caress me
> > I don't need to be held tight.

I only want you to be ready
　　To know my voice will never ring
To know there'll never be another letter
　　You gotta hear this one small thing.

I need you to remember
　　That I never was your shame
I always was your daughter
　　I never did complain.

I always was your daughter
　　I never did complain.

INT. SCHOOL LIBRARY. DAY

We cut to the post-assembly drinks with the parents. They are standing in the library drinking tea and coffee, and there is a rather miserable selection of biscuits being passed round by other members of the sixth form. Teachers are talking in loud, hearty voices to the parents, the Richard III *girl is being made a fuss over.* GIDEON *is pushing his way through the throng towards* NATASHA, *who is at the opposite end of the room surrounded by other girls congratulating her on her performance. We see a girl embrace her laughing and saying goodbye and adding, 'Weird song, Tash . . . !'*

　　GIDEON *reaches* NATASHA *just in time to hear her respond to a question from another girl about what she is going to do now . . . 'Going to take a gap year, are you now, Tash . . . ?'*

NATASHA: Yes, I am pretty sure I am going to take a gap year. Gabby and me are going to do something rather amazing, all being well . . . (*Indicating the dark-haired guitarist.*) . . . We are going to go to South America . . . !

Cries of 'Wow!' from one of the girls.

No, it's better than that, we are going to be working with a conservation group, trying to protect the jaguar

and its habitat . . . It's what I've always wanted to do,
work in conservation . . . We get to go in the jungle
and everything . . . !

GIDEON *has reached her now. We see the surprise in*
GIDEON*'s eyes on hearing this news.*

NATASHA: All being well, it's going to work out . . . (*Laughs.*)
Armed patrols, hacking through the undergrowth . . .
tackling poachers . . . it's fantastic . . . ! Hi, Dad!

GIDEON: Hi . . . (*He smiles, the other girls glancing at him.*)
Great song . . .

NATASHA: Weird, huh . . . ?

GIDEON (*he smiles*): A little surprising, maybe . . .

One of the girls watching giggles . . . 'A French surprise!'

GIDEON *hesitates and then decides that he can't wait to
ask the question. He tries to sound offhand.*

What is this about the jungle? . . . And jaguars?

Voices are calling NATASHA. *She is being tugged at, she is
moving off.*

NATASHA: Got to go and celebrate Dad! . . . See you later.

She begins to disappear in a crowd of excited leavers.

GIDEON: See you.

INT. GIDEON'S APARTMENT. DAY

*A sizeable affluent apartment with large rooms, opening into
each other, so you can see the length of the flat, and its very
high ceilings.*

GIDEON *is sitting on the end of the bed, doing up his shirt,
getting ready for a party.* BARBARA *is in the bathroom in her
underwear, doing her makeup. She stands confidently examining
her face, a moment of self-absorption. She feels good about what
she sees. We cut back to* GIDEON*'s face; we see he is deeply
thoughtful. There is a quick cut of* BILL *pulling the council
leader* PETERSEN *by the hair, her face distorted – a troubling
image of* BILL*'s naked rage and grief.*

BARBARA (*calling from the bathroom*): I know you don't
    want to come to this party . . . but you will love the
    venue . . . It's a really interesting space, I'm sure you
    will want to use it for something –
    We hear a noise. We see NATASHA *enter the flat and make*
    straight for her room, which is right at the other end of the
    flat.
    We cut back to BARBARA *chattering on in the bathroom.*

BARBARA: Do you know, darling, I've counted up nearly
    twenty-seven invitations for us over the next two
    weeks, can you believe it? God knows what I'm going
    to wear to all of them.
    GIDEON *immediately gets up and moves to his daughter's*
    room. NATASHA *greets him with a casual smile.*

NATASHA: Hi, Dad . . . Going out?
    GIDEON *sees the reassuringly girlish decorations in her*
    room are still all in place – posters of movies and pop
    stars. There is no sign of any South American destinations.

GIDEON: Is this a serious idea . . . ? The South American
    jungle?

NATASHA: Sure . . . absolutely.

GIDEON: First I've heard of it.

NATASHA (*casually*): I know . . . It's not arranged yet. When
    it was more definite, I was going to mention it . . .
    GIDEON *trying not to betray his anxiety.*

GIDEON: So it's not definite?

NATASHA (*calm*): Not quite . . . If I get the 'A' grades
    I need – which I won't – I *might* go to Edinburgh . . .
    But I want to do this.
    Then NATASHA *looks up directly at him, as if daring him*
    to make a fuss.
    GIDEON *turns to leave and then stops in the doorway.*
    He tries to sound casual.

GIDEON: As a matter of interest, what were you saying in
    that song? Why did you choose that subject?

NATASHA: I liked it. It was a sad story . . . about love. (*She looks straight at him, holding her look unblinkingly. Her dark eyes.*) It's just a song, Dad.

INT. MODERN GALLERY SPACE. NIGHT
A long, narrow passage winding its way through the gallery space. At the far end there is a strangely-shaped oblong room that we can distantly see but we never reach.

The narrow passage is absolutely crammed with partygoers, sandwiched tightly together as in a surreal train corridor. Along the walls of the passage there are port-holes and we can glimpse more people squashed together through these holes. GIDEON *and* BARBARA *are making their way through the edge of the throng.*

BARBARA *is in a tightly-fitting spangly dress. She looks terrific and on the prowl, her eyes immediately flicking the guests, searching out who precisely is here.*

BARBARA (*chatting to a male guest*): Bruce! Now you're finally in power I hope you're not going to be in too much of a hurry. Still have time to go shopping with me!
GIDEON *looks elegant and seemingly relaxed. He acknowledges the people who greet him with a charming boyish grin. But the camera stays on his face, and as soon as they have passed by we see his thoughtful mood. We begin to see the gathering through his eyes, the fluttering faces, the excited over-confident voices, the clothes and demeanour of 'Cool Britannia'.*

Through the crush he sees DENT *and* SNEATH *together, huddled gossiping.*
SNEATH (*to* GIDEON): Hear you're going to amaze us on Millennium night. Hear even God's going to be impressed – he's going to be forced to watch only us!
GIDEON (*sharp smile to* DENT): Did I say yes to the job? I can't quite remember . . . ?
DENT: Don't start worrying me now!

BARBARA: Of course you did. He tries to pretend it doesn't grab him – but he has been thinking about nothing else! (*She suddenly spies somebody.*) Robert, I don't believe it! Isn't this the third time this week . . . ?!
The young faces in the crammed passage have a slightly ghostly demeanour because of the interesting little white lights in the floor. Suddenly ANDREW *is gesticulating to* GIDEON *down the passage.* GIDEON *moves towards him, past clusters of sharp-faced young women.*

ANDREW: Word is spreading fast . . .

GIDEON (*lightly*): Doesn't it always with you, Andrew?

ANDREW: I've had a call –

GIDEON: From?

ANDREW: I know it's very difficult to surprise you – but this *will* surprise you . . . ! (*He starts pushing his way through the throng.*) We need to find somewhere in private, because this passage has ears! (*He is pushing.*) Follow me . . . (*He pushes hard.*) I think there is a little secret cubicle along here . . .
We cut to GIDEON *glancing at* BARBARA *chatting to a man at the bar.*

BARBARA: A musical about navel cadets, your hopes aren't exactly high, I know. But it was amazing, he played us all the songs right there in his bedroom!
ANDREW *is carving his way through the hallucinatory tightness of the passage.* DIANE, *the starlet, suddenly catches* GIDEON's *arm.*

DIANE: There you are! This is a good moment, isn't it?

GIDEON: A good moment for what?

DIANE (*raising her voice above the chatter*): To decide the next stage of my life! Here goes, anyway – you are not going to escape . . . If I was – and there are *three* stages to this question, because there is a surprise complication coming up – if I was to *accept* . . . you know, to become *the face* of you-know-who . . . I just

wonder . . . of course it will reflect on my image as a
serious actress . . . on the other hand visibility –
visibility beyond the wildest –

*Her voice is cutting out. As she talks, as the words pour
out, her eyes shine with the weight of her problems. But all
we can hear is the surrounding chatter of the party which
is taking on the quality of tinkling glass.*

  DIANE*'s beautiful, self-absorbed face is pushed towards*
GIDEON*'s. As we move in on his eyes, a buzzing begins
and* GIDEON*'s eyes flick for a moment as if he is suffering
from intense claustrophobia. He sees the young faces,*
BARBARA *flirting and gossiping,* ANDREW *is gesturing
towards him from far down the passage to get a move on.*

  Suddenly the sound cuts back with vengeance.

DIANE: So? . . . (*Her eyes studying his face anxiously.*)
Maestro? What do you think?

She stares, desperately eager for his opinion. GIDEON *has
heard absolutely none of what she has said. He decides to
smile sweetly back at her.*

DIANE: So?! (*Her eyes scanning him, searching.*)

GIDEON: So . . . do it. By all means! That's what I say.

DIANE: Do it? (*She beams.*) Really? What *all of it*?! (*Her
face falls, suddenly anxious.*) What about the
complication? . . . You *really* mean do it all?

GIDEON: All of it . . . absolutely! (*He glances towards the
exit, then kisses her.*) Take care, I've just remembered,
I've got to do something . . .

EXT. EDGE OF LONDON. NIGHT

We cut to GIDEON *driving through night streets at the edge of
London, an ethnic mix of people, different clothes, a sense of a
very different city compared to the streets around his office.*

  *He stops his car, in a dark street, where the twenty-four-hour
store is the one exterior which is blazing with light.*

INT. TWENTY-FOUR-HOUR SHOP. NIGHT

GIDEON *enters the convenience store, which is surprisingly large inside. It is full of the usual confectionery, magazines, groceries, a shelf of rather old-looking videos. A couple of late-night shoppers are wandering the aisles, a huge overweight young man in leather and a tense-looking young Asian woman. As* GIDEON *moves among the shelves, he sees* STELLA *dressed in bright clothes standing behind a checkout.* STELLA *calls out to him.*

STELLA: That was quick. (*She laughs.*) I didn't mean you had to bring it back the same day!

GIDEON (*grins*): Well, I thought why not? . . . It gave me a good excuse to leave a fairly horrible party . . .

He hands the video camera to STELLA, *who is watching him closely. He looks very elegant in his evening wear, standing by the crisp packets.*

STELLA: You are giving it back with the tape still in! (*She pulls the tape out.*) Keep it –

GIDEON: It's not worth keeping, I was videoing with the camera round my ankles so as to stop myself being thrown out! – There's nothing really on it . . .

STELLA: You should still keep it – otherwise it was all pointless, wasn't it?!

STELLA pushes the tape towards him. He seems very reluctant to take it, his hand withdrawing.

GIDEON: It isn't worth keeping . . .

STELLA looks straight at him.

STELLA: What did your daughter do at the concert that makes you want to get rid of it as quick as possible?!

The huge boy in leather is watching them from one of the aisles.

GIDEON (*casually*): She sang a song about obsessive love. (*He smiles.*) Don't all school leavers do that at their end-of-term assembly?!

He sees the big boy staring at him. Whispers to STELLA.

You don't mind working all night here? . . . Anybody
could come in . . .

STELLA: And they do . . . ! (*She indicates a tall Asian man
right at the other end of the shop.*) Hanif is here most of
the time . . . He's the boss –
*Hanif is pacing, he seems very wound up, in a world of
his own.*
We shout at each other a lot . . .
GIDEON'*s pager goes off, he looks down and reads the
message and then reluctantly takes out his mobile phone.*
STELLA *watches him read his pager message.*

STELLA: Your wife?

GIDEON: No, I have no wife.

STELLA: Your girlfriend?

GIDEON: No, she's never bothered where I am . . . My
business partner is another matter entirely though!
(*His mobile phone rings, he answers.*) Andrew?
ANDREW *is in the corner of the party, against a white
wall; he is sitting on a floor. There are very few people left
now at the party. We intercut between them.*

ANDREW: Gideon . . . where the hell are you? You
disappeared –

GIDEON: I'm buying sweets . . . (*He finds himself in the
same aisle as the huge boy in leather.*)

ANDREW (*ignoring this*): Where did you go?

GIDEON: I had to do something . . . it was unavoidable.
And then I needed some cheap chocolate –
ANDREW'*s tone changes, suddenly it is hushed and
dramatic.*

ANDREW: Badalamenti wants to see us. He wants to use us!
A flicker of surprise crosses GIDEON'*s face.*

GIDEON: Really?

ANDREW: We're going to be inspected by his foot-soldiers
in a week or so – and then the Man Himself is
coming . . . !

GIDEON: Great.

ANDREW: Come on . . . what's going on here?! You can do better than 'great' . . . (*Suddenly.*) I can't believe you just said 'great' – this is the biggest news we've had – Say something else . . . (*Dangerous smile.*) Say something more than 'great' . . .

GIDEON: I'll call you first thing tomorrow, Andrew. (*He rings off.*)

STELLA: Good news?

GIDEON: One of the biggest media tycoons in the world wants us to represent him . . . It could be worth a lot of money . . . (*He smiles.*) and it will impress people, of course –

STELLA: So it *is* good news?

GIDEON (*grins*): I think it must be, mustn't it? My young partner is very excited –

An old metal alarm clock goes off, ringing busily. GIDEON *turns startled.*

STELLA: It's my break . . . I need a good reminder each night.

GIDEON: Can I . . . ? Can I take you somewhere? For your break –

STELLA (*laughs*): You mean pop along to the nearest four-star restaurant at one a.m. in the morning ?! I don't think so . . . (*She is moving to the corner of the shop, where there is a red door.*) I bring my own provisions . . . tend to tuck in over here . . . (*She's opening the red door.*) I always bring too much – you can have a bite, if you want . . .

INT. DARKENED ROOM. NIGHT
They go through the red door into a large lumber room that adjoins the shop. It is full of clutter: old furniture, dusty old boxes, a pinball machine lying on its side. It is very dark in

there. GIDEON *stops in the doorway staring into the dark and listening to a curious squeaking sound.*

GIDEON: Jesus, what's that noise?

STELLA: The noise? Oh that's a few little rodents, hamsters, guineas . . . you don't mind rodents do you? Hanif and I keep them – as company.

We see four cages of guinea pigs, ornamental rats and hamsters.

    Time cut. STELLA *and* GIDEON *are sitting side by side on the floor in the darkened room, eating sandwiches out of silver foil.* STELLA *has two of the guinea pigs out; one is on her knee, the other is being fed a bit of her salad.*

GIDEON: Terrific sandwich . . . can't see what's in it, but it's great!

STELLA: So what upset you so much on the tape?

GIDEON: Nothing. I just did a lousy job photographing her. Nothing upset me!

STELLA: Well, that's a lie, clearly. (*Lightly.*) But you're not going to tell me any more, so I'll forget it.

GIDEON looks at her, surprised. The rats are rustling in their cage looking at them.

STELLA: So what do you do with all these politicians and VIPs, then? Advise them on their tone of voice, the colour of their clothes, their hair . . . ?

GIDEON: I have done that in my time –

STELLA: Very obedient, are they?

GIDEON: Invariably . . .

We see a quick cut of DENT *with his hair all slicked back. And then we see* DENT *with his hair puffed up, bouffant.* DENT*'s face is extremely anxious, looking for approval for his new image.*

DENT: You must remind me of hand gestures, by the way.

GIDEON laughs at the memory. We cut back to STELLA *watching him.*

GIDEON: I was thinking of one of my old clients . . .

STELLA hands him a guinea pig to hold.

STELLA: Why are you here in the middle of the night?

GIDEON: I needed to bring your camera back . . .

STELLA: If you're still sticking to your story – there's not much point is there – ?

GIDEON flicks this straight back.

GIDEON: Why do *you* work in a twenty-four-hour store?

STELLA (*matter of fact*): Because I lost my child and I split up with my husband and I am afraid to go to bed every night . . . I mean I would have thought that would be really quite simple to work out.

GIDEON: I am sorry . . . That was crass of me . . . (*He looks at her and smiles.*) I just needed to change the subject –

STELLA: It's OK . . . I don't mind. (*Lightly.*) Next time I'll make you answer . . .

GIDEON accidentally lets the guinea pig slip out of his hand. It scuttles off into the dark.

GIDEON: Oh shit, where's it gone . . . I've lost your guinea pig!

STELLA: Come on! We can find it . . . Get on your hands and knees – we'll have to move fast . . . ! There are a lot of places for it to hide . . . .

They are moving in the dark, on all fours, hunting for the guinea pig.

Hanif will be heartbroken if we don't find it!

We stay on GIDEON, crawling behind the shelves, calling out to the guinea pig.

INT. SNEATH'S ROOM. DAY

We cut to SNEATH in close-up.

SNEATH: So . . . the great Gideon Warner, on all fours, looking for a rodent . . . !

He stops, hesitates, looking at BECCA's young face.

Sex . . . Sex is not going to embarrass you is it? If
I describe in detail . . . some sex now?
BECCA *looks at* SNEATH. *She tries not to seem flustered.*
She chooses her words carefully.

BECCA: No, I don't think so . . . (*She hesitates.*) I'll tell you
if it does . . .

SNEATH: Ah . . . ! 'Normal' sex is fine, is that what you
mean? Well in one way, this is pretty normal . . . in
another way it isn't!

BECCA: What do you mean?

SNEATH: This is what I mean –

INT. GIDEON'S BEDROOM. MORNING.

SNEATH (*voice-over*): The beautiful Barbara, a very chilly
person certainly – but she *was* beautiful . . .
We see GIDEON *and* BARBARA *naked together, making*
love. BARBARA*'s face is tilted back, she is having an*
orgasm. As she does so SNEATH*'s matter-of-fact voice-over*
cuts through the image.

SNEATH (*voice-over*): It is Sunday morning . . . and the fact
is, if you think about it, so many people must have
heard the news whilst having sex . . . or just after having
sex. Of all the major extraordinary news stories that
have ever happened – there are very few one can
confidently say that about! But for this one . . . it was
true . . .
We see BARBARA, *face tilted back, as she has her orgasm.*
The telephone is ringing and ringing and ringing.

SNEATH (*voice-over*): Certainly Gideon and Barbara heard
about it while having sex . . .
The phone is still ringing, GIDEON *scrambles across the*
bed and answers the phone.

GIDEON: Andrew? What the hell is it?

We see ANDREW *sitting in his rather austere sitting room, the light of the television playing on his face, but we don't yet see the image on the television screen.*

ANDREW: Switch on the television.

GIDEON: I never switch on the television this early.

ANDREW: You *must* switch on the television.

BARBARA: What is it? What's happened?!

ANDREW: Princess Di, she's been in a car crash. It's really bad!

BARBARA *sits on the end of the bed and switches on the television. We see the images of the crash that killed Princess Diana, the Paris underpass, the very solemn news anchor. As they switch on the television, there is no immediate announcement of her death.*

GIDEON (*into the phone*): Princess Diana? Is she dead? What are they saying?

BARBARA: What? Can I talk to him?

BARBARA *almost snatches the phone. Her manner is urgent, eager for news. She stands naked in front of the television staring at the image and talking to* ANDREW *excitedly. We intercut between them.*

BARBARA: Is she dead . . . have they said she is dead?

ANDREW: They've just said she died, they have just announced it.

BARBARA: Good Lord, how extraordinary . . . This is the end of Charles, *surely*!

ANDREW: Absolutely, absolutely. I agree totally.

BARBARA: She's dead?! God, what will this mean? I think it means the end of Charles . . . (*She is kneeling, still naked, right up to the image on the television.*) What happened? Where were the bodyguards? The press were chasing, were they? It's amazing! Just when you think you know where everything is heading . . . I can't believe it! What are you on, one or three?

GIDEON *stares in disbelief at* BARBARA, *naked in front of the television, really energised by the news.*
We cut back to SNEATH.

SNEATH: Before we are too harsh on her – I have to admit I reacted just like she did!

INT. GIDEON'S OFFICE. DAY
We cut to GIDEON, *in his office, swivelling slightly in his chair, staring out of his window. He can see a series of very different people carrying flowers on the pavement. The woman with the tiny dogs carrying a huge bouquet, two children struggling along with a vast array of flowers that is almost as big as them. A car absolutely full of flowers draws up and two young men jump out and start laying flowers along the wall.*

Suddenly we cut wide and see that GIDEON'*s office is crammed full of people – different European faces, Italians, French, Greek. A central* SPOKESMAN *is sitting opposite* GIDEON; *he is in full flood.* ANDREW *is watching the whole procedure very carefully.*

BADALAMENTI'S SPOKESMAN: Mr Badalamenti will want the agenda to be very clear next week – the questions about foreign ownership, the questions on the percentage size of the market, the questions about digital penetration –

ANDREW: Sure . . . absolutely!

BADALAMENTI'S SPOKESMAN: Mr Badalamenti will wish to see definite replies to all these questions before the meeting . . . !
GIDEON *can only very faintly hear what he is saying. Instead he is watching the people carrying the flowers. Suddenly* ANDREW'*s voice is cutting through.*

ANDREW: Gideon?!
GIDEON *turns; all the faces are staring at him, waiting for*

a reply. ANDREW *is staring straight into* GIDEON*'s eyes.*
GIDEON *smiles.*

GIDEON: You know I think every florist, every flower
barrow in the whole city must be empty . . . Maybe
that's true all over Europe! Can you ever remember a
time when that has ever happened before . . . ?
They are all looking at him blankly. Then GIDEON *adopts
a magisterial manner.*
I understand everything you say, gentlemen. (*He leans
forward, confidentially.*) Everything.

EXT. THE EDGE OF A LONDON PARK. DAY
*We cut to the camera moving over flowers, a carpet of flowers
on the ground, and then we see flowers tied to the park fence
and then we see* GIDEON *moving among the flowers. Long-lens
shot of people laying them on the ground. A young teenage girl
is hurling rose petals in the air and they float for a moment in
the breeze. We suddenly see* BILL*'s bulky shape walking towards
us, glimpsed through a shower of falling rose petals.* GIDEON *can't
stop himself looking a tiny bit apprehensive as* BILL *approaches.*
BILL *is picking up spare flowers, breaking them off other
people's bunches, forming a large mixed posy of his own.*
BILL *sees* GIDEON *looking tense at his approach. He smiles
at* GIDEON.

BILL: Don't worry – I am not at full throttle today . . . !
GIDEON: I am sorry that it wasn't a complete success –
the demonstration . . .
BILL: It had its moments. For me anyway! I will be at
them again of course . . . (*He looks at his flowers.*) Just
collecting a few . . . for the cycle lane – for my son! . . .
They won't miss a few from here, will they . . . ?
BILL *looks anxiously at* GIDEON, *wanting his approval.*
GIDEON: No, they won't . . .

He watches BILL *move off, as he disappears among the people in the park, his bulky shape seen through more falling rose petals.*

INT. GIDEON'S FLAT. DAY

We cut to BARBARA *and* GIDEON *watching Diana's cortège after the funeral, making its way out of London, on the television. The astonishing images of people throwing flowers on the hearse from the side of dual carriageways, from motorway bridges, from the top of multi-storey car parks. The vehicle's bonnet is clouded with flowers, so the windscreen wipers have to try to get rid of some of them, the edge of the motorway is becoming coated in flowers.*

The phone rings. ANDREW *is on his mobile in the street.*

ANDREW: I had to come over . . . Can I come in Gideon? I have to see it with you!

GIDEON: That was Andrew. He wants to watch it with us.

BARBARA *mutters, she is staring transfixed at the television screen.*

EXT. STREET WITH CYCLE LANE. DAY

We see BILL *alone in the road laying a carpet of flowers along the cycle lane where his son died, whistling in a rather anarchic fashion as he does so.*

INT. GIDEON'S FLAT. DAY

We cut to the television screen. The cortège has moved further along the motorway with people lining the road, throwing their flowers.

ANDREW *is sitting in front of the television on the floor, like a child, really close to the screen.*

ANDREW: Amazing isn't it, absolutely amazing!

BARBARA: Extraordinary, I have never seen anything like it before . . . It's like from another century!

ANDREW (*getting even closer to the screen*): You're going to yell at me for this, Gideon . . . but this is because of *you*.

GIDEON (*astonished*): Because of *me*?!

ANDREW: Sure . . . the flowers two years ago, across the city – subconsciously that set this up . . . the flowers pouring down . . . you started this!

We see the images on the screen.

This is you . . . !

GIDEON: Jesus, Andrew, whatever will you be crediting me with next?

ANDREW *looks up at him from the floor.*

ANDREW: It's a scary thought, I know – but it's true . . .

There is a noise. GIDEON *sees* NATASHA *re-entering the flat.*

GIDEON: There you are! I thought you would be watching this –

NATASHA: I've been out in the street . . . it's a little hysterical out there.

She goes into her room. GIDEON *follows her as* BARBARA *and* ANDREW *stare mesmerised at the television.*

GIDEON *stops in the doorway. The decorations on* NATASHA's *bedroom wall have changed: there are now images of South America and plenty of pictures of jaguars.*

GIDEON: Have you definitely decided? . . . Your plans?

NATASHA *is curled up on the end of the bed. She hardly moves.*

NATASHA (*calmly*): I think so.

GIDEON: Are you going to tell me your A-level results . . . ?

NATASHA *just stares at him; she refuses to reply.* GIDEON *can see an envelope poking out of her books.*

GIDEON: For Chrissake, it has been days . . . no other parent doesn't know his daughter's A-level results!!

NATASHA (*reluctantly*): I got three 'A's.

GIDEON: That's terrific, that's fantastic darling . . . ! (*He moves to kiss her.*)

NATASHA: I'm still going. (*She stares straight at him.*) To the jungle . . .

GIDEON: Which is where?

NATASHA: Where the scheme is. Which is in Colombia.

GIDEON: Colombia?! Jesus, Natasha, that is the most dangerous country in the world . . .

NATASHA: I will be with people –

GIDEON: Of course you will be with people! –

NATASHA: Don't push me Dad . . . That's the quickest way to –

GIDEON: Don't push you . . . ! What will you do?! (*She keeps looking at him unblinkingly.*) Will you at least keep your place at Edinburgh open while I research this scheme . . . ? Will you do that?

NATASHA *does not react.*

GIDEON: Will you do that for me?

We hear BARBARA *and* ANDREW *in the background exclaiming at the things they see on the screen.*

ANDREW: This is amazing . . . this is pure Gideon . . . a snowstorm of white daises! (*He calls.*) Come and look at this, Gideon . . .

GIDEON (*staring at* NATASHA): Will you do that at least?

NATASHA: I'll think about it. (*Her dark eyes fixing him implacably.*)

INT. GIDEON'S OFFICE. MORNING

We cut to GIDEON *sitting alone in his office, early morning light. On the television screen we can see the tape of* NATASHA *singing her song, her face is on the edge of the frame, sliced in half. We can only see one eye, though we can hear the song clearly.* GIDEON *stares at the one eye staring back at him. The song*

pours out, plaintive and accusatory. We move in on GIDEON's
face as he sits absolutely still, listening to his daughter's song.

INT. GIDEON'S BOARDROOM. DAY
Several of the young members of GIDEON's *staff are sitting
round the boardroom table waiting for him.* ANDREW *is sitting
at the far end of the table facing the door.* GIDEON *takes out his
mobile phone as he approaches the room. He dials rapidly. We
intercut with* STELLA *cleaning out the guinea pigs' cages in the
lumber room next to the shop.*

STELLA: Hello? Good morning, you just caught me deep
in guinea-pig shit . . .

GIDEON: Can you call me on my mobile in precisely three
minutes? . . . *Please.* I need you to do this – in
precisely three minutes . . .

STELLA (*hesitates for a moment*): Yes . . .

GIDEON *enters the boardroom.*

ANDREW: There you are!

GIDEON *sits at the head of the table. All the eager young
faces staring at him.*

GIDEON: Good morning, everyone . . . (*He puts his mobile
phone down on the table in front of him; for a second he
stares at it. He suddenly looks up at* ANDREW.) Why
don't you kick off, Andrew, tell us what's important
this week . . .

ANDREW *is startled; he is watching* GIDEON's *strange
manner.*

ANDREW: Well, I think everybody here knows perfectly
well this is a big week . . .

GIDEON (*staring at the phone*): Go on. Tell us a little more.

ANDREW: Well, obviously it's not just big because we
have got Badalamenti here today – actually in these
offices – but it's big because of where it's going to
lead. We are a very influential but *small* firm . . . (*He*

is looking straight at GIDEON, *his tone very pointed.*)
Hand-crafted, of course beautiful – but a miniature.
Now we have a chance to become a much bigger
concern . . . with everything that's happening –
GIDEON *can't take his eyes of the mobile. It is not ringing.*
ANDREW *is watching him and speaking directly to him.*

ANDREW: Instead of running the risk of being swallowed
by some bigger outfit . . . we will – however indelicate
this sounds – be doing the swallowing ourselves. We
have that chance – which starts this week, *nothing
must get in the way of that.*
The phone lies silent. The buzzing is starting. GIDEON *is
desperate to leave.*

GIDEON: You take the words . . . you take the words right
out of my . . .
*He stops. He is staring at the phone willing it to ring.
Suddenly it rings.* GIDEON *forces himself not to grab it,
but to pick it up leisurely.*

GIDEON (*into phone*): Thank you. Yes, that's interesting
news. I understand. I'll come at once – if that's what
you want. (*He rings off and looks up.*) Sorry, something
has come up . . . I thought it might – and it has . . .
ANDREW *watches him very beadily as he leaves.*

ANDREW: You'll be back for the pre-Badalamenti briefing
in two hours . . . ?

GIDEON (*stopping in the doorway*): Naturally. What do you
take me for?

EXT. EDGE OF LONDON, STREETS. DAY
We see GIDEON *in his Mercedes driving the streets we saw
before, on the edge of London, but this time by daylight.*
    STELLA *is standing in the middle of the pavement in the
High Street waiting for him. She is wearing her bright vibrant
colours, a little brash, a little eccentric.*

GIDEON (*lowering the window*): Jump in . . . I'll take you
wherever you want to eat . . . doesn't matter where it is!

STELLA: No, you jump out, because we are eating over
there!

GIDEON *staring across in surprise at an Indian/Malaysian/
Thai restaurant with a dodgy-looking sign: 'Star of the
Orient'.*

GIDEON: We're going in there?! Are you sure?

INT. STAR OF THE ORIENT. DAY

We cut to GIDEON *and* STELLA *entering the interior of the
restaurant. It is very large, full of over-the-top décor –
ornamental red elephant heads, gold and white everywhere.*

GIDEON: Jesus, it's enormous! (*He stares at the rows of
empty tables.*) Not exactly busy, though –

STELLA: I've eaten here once before . . . it was amazing. But
business is obviously a little erratic at the moment . . .

Time cut. GIDEON *and* STELLA *are eating now, small
delicate helpings of hors d'oeuvres.*

GIDEON (*surprised tone*): This is delicious . . .

STELLA: Told you so.

GIDEON (*pointing at the little dishes*): And I like small
helpings . . .

*He glances up at the owner, who is beaming at them across
the large empty restaurant, and the waiters who are
watching them eat.*

The décor is truly –

STELLA (*laughing*): Bonkers . . . ! I love it!

GIDEON *smiles at her infectious laugh.* STELLA *looks
directly at him.*

STELLA: Why did I have to make that call to get you out
of that meeting?

GIDEON: I wanted to see you . . . (*Nonchalantly.*) I needed
to see you urgently . . .

STELLA: And that's your normal method is it? For inviting
people out? (*She imitates him.*) 'Phone me back in
three minutes without fail!' (*Lightly.*) I told you this
time you've gotta answer me . . . gotta tell the truth.

GIDEON (*grins, trying to deflect her*): That's asking a lot,
I am in PR, after all.

STELLA (*smiles thinly at this*): You know I was thinking
about you when I was cleaning out the guinea pigs'
poo – before you rang me in fact – I was thinking
where I would fit in . . . You know, those groups you
do, I'm sure you do them all the time – focus groups.
I was wondering if I would ever get on one. Would
somebody like me ever get selected? (*She looks up and
grins.*) Try giving a straight answer to that!

GIDEON: It's possible – (*He smiles, staring at her eccentric
clothes.*) You might cross over too many categories . . .

STELLA: You bet! Don't fit any categories, do I . . . ?! One
look at me – this woman is a little crazy, get her out of
here . . . ! But you know I really do believe everybody
is like me . . . Yes! I mean . . . you look at people in
the street – have you ever really *looked* at people as
they walk by?!

GIDEON *smiles.*

STELLA: There are so many really strange characters out
there. I mean – weird faces . . . *different* . . . People
never look like what they're meant to look like, don't
you think? Do you get what I mean? They're larger . . .
or tinier . . . but not the sort of medium-sized
shrivelled-up blank sort of people – like I bet you
have in your groups . . . they're the weird ones!
They're the aliens . . .

*We see a wide shot of them eating amongst the surreal
décor.*

GIDEON: They're always very carefully researched those
groups . . . on a scientific basis –

STELLA: 'Scientific basis'? (*She laughs.*) Oh come on,
    Gideon . . . ! (*She looks at him.*) Think about it next
    time you've got your nose pressed up to the two-way
    mirror . . . think about this meal!
    GIDEON *smiles at this. There is a noise and he looks*
    around, to see a mighty trolley of food bearing down on
    them. And the waiters descending holding still more dishes.

GIDEON: How many people have you ordered for, Stella?!

STELLA: We'll eat it all, don't worry. (*To the owner.*) Done
    your best to impress, have you? Because this man here
    could do you some good!
    The owner beams.
    Could get you some great PR . . . so I hope you've got
    all your absolute star dishes here!

EXT. SUBURBAN STREETS. DAY

We cut to STELLA *and* GIDEON *moving across a little suburban*
park, both of them walking gingerly, having eaten far too much.

GIDEON: I don't think I have been so full . . . ever! I never
    eat much . . . I feel I've swallowed . . . I've consumed –
    (*He stops for a moment, breathing heavily.*) something . . .
    extremely *large* . . .

STELLA: A brisk walk will help matters . . . (*She turns.*)
    And *then* what happens?

GIDEON: What do you mean?

STELLA: And *then* what happens? That's what I mean.
    Do you want to see where I live . . . ?

GIDEON: I have this incredibly important meeting – I have
    to return to – with this media tycoon I told you about
    . . . the pre-meeting briefing starts in ten minutes.

STELLA: In ten minutes!? You're going to be pushed to
    make it, then.

GIDEON: This is true . . .
    They face each other in the suburban park.

STELLA: So goodbye, then.

GIDEON (*hesitates*): I can always skip the pre-briefing . . .

INT. STELLA'S HOUSE. DAY

We cut to them entering STELLA's *little suburban house, the same as millions of others on the edge of London. As soon as they get through the door* GIDEON *sees there is very little décor in the house. The largest room, the sitting room, is totally bare except for a mattress on the floor which has a rather nice bed cover draped over it. The ceiling has clouds painted on it. There are speakers in the room and no other chairs or decoration.*

    GIDEON *sees the mattress and hesitates in the doorway.*

STELLA (*laughs*): Don't look like that . . . I'm not going to leap on you! This is what I do after a night at work . . . I lie here, look at the ceiling, listen to some great music . . . and then see what happens . . . I try to think of different things each day . . . things I've seen . . . or read about. Try to surprise myself, keep the mind occupied . . . so I don't *dwell*.

GIDEON: I understand –

STELLA (*imitating him*): 'I understand' . . . You don't look very happy about it! (*She puts some music on.*) I usually have a bit of baroque –

    A baroque trumpet concerto bursts out.

    Then I usually flop down here . . . (*She hesitates, then laughs.*) But maybe not today . . . !

    She sits on the edge of the mattress decorously. GIDEON *is still in the doorway; he crouches down to be on the same level as her.*

GIDEON: This is how you spend all your time during the day? Shut in here?

STELLA: Well, sometimes I have a complete change of

scene – I go and listen to a friend of mine sing in a
church choir in Wolverhampton!

GIDEON: Right . . . (*He grins.*) I can see that would make
for a complete change of scene, yes!

STELLA: Bet you haven't been in a house like this for a
long time?

GIDEON: Oh, don't be so sure . . . I grew up not so far
away from here – in a house just like this.

STELLA: Really?! (*She looks at his elegant appearance and his
posh voice.*) That would have taken some guessing . . .
I grew up round here too – that's why I've come back.
(*She lies back on the mattress, staring at the ceiling.*) I'm
just lying down because it's my usual routine. (*She
smiles.*) Got to keep to it . . . That means – if you
grew up here – we probably passed each other as
children . . . that's a thought! My father kept a
chemist shop . . . in Randolph Road . . . You might
have come in there . . . Did you ever come in there?

FLASHBACK. CHEMIST SHOP INTERCUT WITH STELLA'S
ROOM. DAY
*We see the huge old coloured-water vessels, bright blues and reds
and greens, that dominated old chemist shops – enormous glass
bottles with coloured water. A fifteen-year-old boy walks through
the dark shop towards a man in a white coat.*

STELLA (*voice-over*): You may have come in to buy some
condoms from my dad . . . your first ever condoms.

YOUNG GIDEON: Um, um, can I have a packet of cough
lozenges please?
We cut back to GIDEON, *smiling.*

GIDEON: That's a great thought . . . but I don't think I ever
bought condoms from round here. But I remember
those old chemist shops – whatever was that coloured
water for?

We see the boy's face reflected in the giant bottles.

    GIDEON *lies down cautiously on the side of the mattress, staring up at the ceiling. They are now lying side by side. The music is playing.* STELLA *turns to look at him, challenging him to tell her something.*

GIDEON: My father was a chauffeur . . . he was Polish, never spoke very good English – This ludicrous name, 'Gideon Warner', should be Gideon Wojtalavicz.

STELLA: I like that . . . !

FLASHBACK. INT. PERIOD CAR / STELLA'S ROOM. DAY

We see a man in his forties driving a large old Daimler with a little boy sitting in the front seat watching his FATHER *drive. We intercut between* GIDEON *now and his voice-over across the images.*

GIDEON: We travelled all over the place . . . making it more difficult for you and me to have crossed . . .

STELLA: Go on though – you rode with him in the big cars, I like that . . . Sometimes I got to go in those old Daimlers, at weddings and things . . . The smell of the leather – I still smell it sometimes . . .

    We see the boy in the front seat next to his FATHER, *as his* FATHER *drives the big car.*

GIDEON: My father sometimes managed to get me along for the ride . . .

    We cut to little GIDEON *sitting in the front seat of a limousine watching his* FATHER *drive the car. His* FATHER *is dressed in a chauffeur's livery.*

GIDEON'S FATHER: I shall show you their houses too. At least from the outside – just when they are switching on all their lights, and you will watch these people go in and out and you can dream about what they're going to do.

We see the little boy's face staring at his FATHER *and then at the big houses with their lights just turning on, their rich interiors glowing out.*

STELLA: You saw lots of different people? . . . I can imagine it –

We see a small girl riding in the back of the car, as STELLA *imagines herself as part of* GIDEON's *past.*

GIDEON: Sure . . . I saw lots of important people of those days. I remember a great time once . . . my father was driving a member of the House of Lords who was also in the Tory cabinet or shadow cabinet, I forget. And we went down to the country, they were all taking part in a fishing competition would you believe . . . All these important grandees.

FLASHBACK. EXT. PERIOD CARS. RIVER / STELLA'S ROOM. DAY

We see a line of Daimlers and Armstrong Sidleys parked side by side, with old Tory grandees putting on their Wellington boots as they sit on the edge of the cars.

Then we see the boy staring down on them all as they fish in total silence.

We cut back to STELLA, *her face staring close to* GIDEON.

STELLA: I love that . . . all these old farts fishing!

GIDEON: Sometimes I wonder if I dreamt it . . . because they seemed so unhurried, so silent. They were all politicians . . . but everything was so leisurely! They were a pretty eccentric bunch . . . when you got really close . . . God, they were strange . . .

We see the little girl staring down at them too, at these oddly shaped grandees fishing. Their peculiar glassy stare: they look quite like subterranean creatures themselves.

STELLA: I can just imagine!

We cut back to GIDEON *staring at her in the present.*

GIDEON: I must go.

STELLA: Go on then.

GIDEON: If I miss this meeting – I will have blown everything . . .

STELLA: Off you go, then.

Their faces are very close.

GIDEON: I just . . . would like to tell you something else . . .
You might remember this a bit as well . . . (*Lightly.*)
You see I'm really a complete and utter fraud, Stella,
because I am not this special guru at all – this piss-
elegant world authority! I was once just a really
ordinary nuts-and-bolts PR guy handling some old
seventies comedians after they fell on hard times in the
eighties . . . you will remember some of their names,
probably . . . people like Crumb and Yardley . . .
Miller and Dave . . . remember them?

FLASHBACK. INT. COACH / STELLA'S ROOM. DAY
*We see a coach full of seventies comedians rolling along, a
younger-looking* GIDEON *moving amongst them as the coach
travels, joking with them.*

We cut back to STELLA.

STELLA: Of course – I used to scream! I used to wet
myself when they were on!

*We cut back inside the smoke-filled coach. A podgy man,
Miller, is telling jokes on the coach microphone, trying to
entertain his fellow-comedians as they travel to the next
venue.*

GIDEON (*voice-over*): Miller, of Miller and Dave, was always
on, even when we were travelling! I was getting them
gigs in panto, trying to keep them in the public eye. I
was just in minor showbiz . . . going from gig to gig.
*We see the comedians drinking and eating on the coach,
chain-smoking.*

I wanted to run as far away as possible from those old
politicians that my father used to drive . . . amazingly,
it led me straight back to them – through a whole
series of odd connections and unexpected breaks –
We cut back to GIDEON *in the present.*
If I don't go now I'll miss the meeting, and I *can't*
miss the meeting . . . it'll be a disaster.

STELLA: Go then. You must go, Gideon.

GIDEON (*quietly*): I can't go . . . (*We see the vulnerability in
his eyes.*)

STELLA: Why is your daughter angry with you? She is
angry with you, isn't she?

GIDEON: Yes . . . (*He hesitates.*) It's to do with my wife.

FLASHBACK. INT. HOSPITAL / STELLA'S ROOM. DAY
*We see the camera moving along a passage in a private hospital
ward, snaking round past the small cubicle rooms, until it comes
to rest on one particular room.*

We cut back to GIDEON, *lying next to* STELLA *on the mattress.
Her face close.*

STELLA: Did your wife die?

GIDEON: Yes, of cancer . . . We'd been estranged for some
years, we were living apart . . . I'd been unfaithful –
(*He suddenly adds:*) Not horrendously! . . . Certainly
not hundreds and hundreds –

STELLA (*laughs*): I should hope not! –

GIDEON: No, no, I'll explain about that some other time –
my daughter's song . . . Anyway it was nothing like
that –

STELLA: You mean just the bog-standard average for the
male executive –

GIDEON (*thinking for a moment, slight laugh*): Possibly
more than that . . . I don't know . . . Anyway, this is
just a very strange little thing . . . I mean I *had* been

attentive, visiting – my wife was very near the end,
you know, nobody was quite certain when she was
going to go . . . would it be this evening, would it be
tomorrow morning –

We move in on his eyes, close. We cut to GIDEON *sitting
with his wife, a dark-haired woman lying in the bed,
staring at him as she breathes with difficulty. And a young*
NATASHA *sits in the corner, aged about twelve.*

GIDEON (*voice-over*): I'm sitting there . . . sometimes
thinking about my girlfriends – that's not such a
betrayal, I don't think . . .

We see NATASHA *glancing across at him.*

GIDEON: I mean, you know, clutching out for the living . . .
it's ruthless . . . but sort of natural maybe . . .

We see a younger BARBARA *staring at him, her eyes wide;
he's touching her lips. We cut back to* GIDEON *in the
present. He hesitates.*

GIDEON: It's such a small thing really . . . what happened . . .

STELLA: Go on . . .

We cut back to the hospital room and passages.

GIDEON (*voice-over*): For some bizarre reason . . . you
know how there are always people wandering about
hospitals . . . anyway, somehow there was this bloke,
in a funny old mackintosh and with a little suitcase,
and he came and sat down in our small room . . . as
my wife was dying . . . He was a total stranger, said
a few things about the weather! –

We see the man sitting with his suitcase.

He was mildly odd – it was quite difficult to get rid
of him, but eventually I did. And then for some
reason . . . some overpowering reason – I needed to
make some calls to just be out of there –

*We see him in the passage chatting away on a coin-box
phone.*

I was in the passage . . . and I made some calls – to
work, to a girlfriend . . . it may have been Barbara, it
may not have been . . . There are people running
backwards and forwards around me.
We see them flit past.
I take no notice . . .
We see GIDEON *moving back into the small room.*
I go back, the funny man is sitting there, my wife
Ellen has gone – she's died *and I was on the phone.* But
this man has come back in his mackintosh, and she's
died with a stranger, sitting there next to Natasha –
the nurses thought he was family! And apparently
I had been on the phone for over half an hour . . .
maybe much more . . . maybe over an hour . . . I let
him come back, I wasn't there . . .
We see the young NATASHA *staring at her father.*

GIDEON: Natasha has never forgiven me . . .
The young NATASHA *is staring straight into* GIDEON*'s
eyes. We cut back to* GIDEON *and* STELLA.

STELLA (*gently, softly, she kisses him once*): She's not
punishing you for that –

GIDEON: No, for what went before . . . I know . . . (*He's
looking at* STELLA.) But I've lost her . . . probably for
ever.

STELLA: I doubt that.
We see an image of NATASHA, *as she is now, staring at him.*

GIDEON: I think you'll find I have. (*For a moment he can't
move.*) I can't believe I missed this meeting! And it's a
completely impossible situation for me to talk myself
out of . . .

STELLA (*touching him*): Just tell them you've been
sampling the best cuisine in London – at the Star of
the Orient . . .
*She kisses him. A high shot of the bare little room as they
kiss passionately.*

INT. GIDEON'S OFFICES. DAY

We cut to GIDEON *moving through his office, all his young staff are staring at him – surprised, awkward, not knowing what to say.* ANDREW *suddenly appears by* GIDEON's *side, his voice an intense whisper.*

ANDREW: What on earth happened to you, Gideon?!

GIDEON: Traffic.

ANDREW: Traffic?!

GIDEON: Yes, traffic.

> ANDREW *physically stops* GIDEON *moving through his office. He stands in front of him, his face close.*

ANDREW: How on earth did you know?

GIDEON: Know what? Why are you whispering?

ANDREW (*even quieter whisper*): I think you *knew* before you left, didn't you?

> GIDEON *suddenly looks up and sees there are foreign-looking bodyguards standing all over his office. The whole floor is bristling with them.*

> *Slowly* GIDEON *starts moving through the office, a floating camera movement, as he approaches his inner office.* ANDREW *is all the time whispering in his ear.*

ANDREW: If you knew he was going to be two hours late, why didn't you tell us . . . ?! It amazes me he hasn't left yet . . . He's been here a quarter of an hour already . . . !

> GIDEON *is moving past the last bodyguard and into his inner office. Subjective shot reveals his office crammed with an entourage of advisers, and sitting in the chair directly facing* GIDEON's *desk is a tiny Italian man drinking a glass of water. At first we only see the back of his head.*

> *As* GIDEON *enters his office all the associates' eyes flash in his direction.*

> *The tiny Italian man,* BADALAMENTI, *flicks his head round with an abrupt movement.*

BADALAMENTI: A man who is even later than me . . .

GIDEON *smiles graciously, but does not apologise. He sits behind his grand desk.*

GIDEON: Good evening, gentlemen . . . (*As if nothing has happened.*) So here we all are . . .

BADALAMENTI *is staring at him with dark eyes, an intimidating look that is unwavering.* GIDEON *smiles back at him, then cannot stop himself sneaking a look out of the window. The large lady is walking her tiny dogs; she is dressed for the first time in a vivid pink dress.*

BADALAMENTI'S SPOKESMAN: You will tell Mr Badalamenti first about what you have discovered concerning the rules of ownership – if one is not a resident of the United Kingdom – the rules that apply to owning commercial television channels. How these may change with this new government. And secondly –

BADALAMENTI *holds up his hand. The* SPOKESMAN *immediately falls silent.*

BADALAMENTI: We do not do secondly yet.

GIDEON *tries not to look at the great pink woman walking her dogs.* BADALAMENTI *is leaning forwards and says something to* GIDEON.

BADALAMENTI: Firstly, *I* have one question . . .

We are on GIDEON*'s eyes. There is a quick cut of* STELLA *staring at him on the mattress, her face close to his. The buzzing is starting on the soundtrack.* BADALAMENTI *is leaning forward saying something to* GIDEON, *but he cannot hear what he is saying for a few seconds. He can see the associates all watching,* ANDREW *staring at him very closely from the doorway.* BADALAMENTI *has stopped talking, he is looking directly into* GIDEON*'s eyes. The sound cuts back abruptly. Everybody is looking at* GIDEON.

BADALAMENTI: I repeat – the WIND?!

GIDEON *looks blank.* BADALAMENTI *points at the photographs with all the flowers falling.*

BADALAMENTI: How did you know there was no big wind
  coming, that it wouldn't blow all your pretty flowers
  away?
GIDEON (*nonchalantly*): That was easy. That was simple.
  I paid God.
  There is a faint smile from BADALAMENTI. *His eyes are*
  piercing into GIDEON'*s as if he has rumbled him.*
BADALAMENTI: I need to make a phone call – *in private.*
  All the associates begin to move in unison.
  No – (BADALAMENTI *stands up.*) I need a room on my
  own. But not this room. (*Another piercing look at*
  GIDEON.) Maybe you could be so kind to find one
  for me . . .
GIDEON: Sure.

INT. OUTER OFFICES. EVENING
GIDEON *moving with* BADALAMENTI *through the offices. All*
the associates and ANDREW *are crowded at the far end.*
GIDEON'*s staff are all standing watching.* GIDEON *opens a*
door to a small conference room. BADALAMENTI *takes the*
briefest of looks and shakes his head.
BADALAMENTI: No, please. This is no good. Another!
  They move off. GIDEON *offering another small office,*
  BADALAMENTI *rejects this one too. They are now almost*
  out on the landing. GIDEON *casually suggests the*
  crammed kitchen area. BADALAMENTI *immediately*
  moves in there. They are now completely out of sight of the
  bodyguards, the associates, and GIDEON'*s staff.*
  BADALAMENTI *turns dangerously in the very confined*
  kitchen space. He jabs his finger into GIDEON'*s chest.*
BADALAMENTI: You're late for me! Nobody knows where
  you are . . . your staff try to lie – but do it very badly!
  And when we start to talk – you don't LISTEN . . .
  A worse listener even than me . . . ! (*He jabs his*

finger.) It has been many years, many many years, since somebody not listened when I speak!

GIDEON *stands staring down at the tiny man poking him.*

GIDEON: So? I am here now, aren't I?

BADALAMENTI *suddenly reaches up and puts both of his hands on* GIDEON's *shoulders, holding onto him in a disconcerting fashion.*

BADALAMENTI: You have the same idea as me! The only person I have met – never listen to what the idiots say *first* . . . if it's any good they will say it again! (*He grins.*) I love it! (*He tightens his grip.*) I do love it! I think you are what I need. (*He tightens his grip.*) You *are* what I need.

GIDEON *staring down in a deadpan fashion at the tiny man with his sudden demented enthusiasm.*

INT. SNEATH'S ROOM. DAY
We cut back to SNEATH. *Big close-up.*

SNEATH: Amazing . . . If you don't care, if you're not afraid, see what happens . . . As long as you're not found out.

EXT. LONDON STREET. EVENING
We cut to GIDEON *driving in his Mercedes that same evening. The light is just dipping, it is on the edge of dusk. He suddenly sees through the windscreen* NATASHA *walking briskly along the street near their apartment, her shoulders hunched, deep in thought.*

GIDEON *begins to follow her, driving very slowly, keeping just slightly behind her.*

NATASHA *suddenly turns round and sees her father in the car.*

NATASHA: Dad? (*She comes up to the car, which has stopped. She looks suspicious.*) What are you doing following me?

GIDEON: I wasn't following you. I was just drifting.

NATASHA: Just drifting, were you?

GIDEON: We both were. Come on, get in for a moment.

NATASHA: Get in the car?

GIDEON (*trying to keep his tone light*): What do you mean,
'Get in the car?' (*He smiles.*) Never in the car with
strangers! – Is that what it's like? Come on, just for a
minute. Why not? I'll give you a lift –

NATASHA: I'm going to meet some friends – I've got to –

GIDEON: I'll drive you wherever you want, please.

> *We cut to them together in the car as* GIDEON *drives
> through an evening London. Driving his daughter in the
> big Mercedes.* NATASHA *opens her window, leans back in
> her seat, her eyes half-closed.*
>
> GIDEON *keeps giving her little glances as he drives.*

GIDEON: I used to do this with my dad . . . drive across
the city . . . just at this time, just when everybody was
switching on their lights. You can see into people's
lives . . . stare at their work . . . You see all sorts of
things.

> *We see the lighted interiors glowing out, some rather grand
> rooms in a central London terrace. A cluster of silhouetted
> figures, some other people arguing.*

This is a good part of town to do it in . . .

> NATASHA *is leaning back in her seat. She is not looking
> out of the window.*
>
> GIDEON *suddenly stops the car. He looks at her. He
> touches her arm.*

GIDEON: Don't go . . . don't go away. PLEASE!

> NATASHA *turns to look at him calmly, very detached.*

NATASHA: I'm going to be late. (*She gets out of the car, and
turns to speak to him through the window.*) There's a
deadline. I will let you know when the deadline has
passed.

> *She moves off, disappearing into the dusk. We stay on*
> GIDEON's *anxious face.*

INT. SNEATH'S ROOM. DAY

We cut to BECCA*'s young face, her big eyes staring enquiringly.*
SNEATH *watching her for a second.*

SNEATH: The power that a child has over one . . . You're
too young Becca . . . to know what it's like to be on
the receiving end.

BECCA (*quietly*): I can understand . . . (*She looks
concerned.*) Does she keep to the deadline? . . . Does
she hurt him?

SNEATH *looks at* BECCA, *surprised by her concern.*

SNEATH: It's the day of a very big meeting with the
government –

EXT. EDGE OF WOLVERHAMPTON. DAY

We see a wide shot of GIDEON *and* STELLA *crossing some waste
ground near some decaying industrial buildings on the edge of
Wolverhampton. A large stark landscape, the two figures
dwarfed by the buildings.*

SNEATH (*voice-over*): And the day of the deadline. It's
funny how often things come together on the same
day, isn't it. So where do we find Gideon first thing
in the morning on this big day? . . . Wandering with
Stella on the outskirts of some godforsaken place –
apparently to take his mind off things. Nobody knows
about Stella . . . nobody has seen them together.

GIDEON: I can't believe I've done this!

STELLA: Why? What's the problem?

GIDEON *is reluctantly moving up the hill, past a
particularly vivid wreck of a building.*

STELLA: You need to get out of London once in a while . . .
if you are going to sell the whole country on
Millennium night –

GIDEON: Well, this would be a challenge certainly – to sell
this . . . ! There aren't meant to be places like this left –

(*He stops and checks his phone.*)

STELLA: Checking to see if there are any messages from
her?

GIDEON: No, she won't let me know till much later. I bet
the deadline goes to the end of the day . . . It was bad
enough waiting for her exam results! Do exams ever
leave one? You think you've left it all behind when you
become 'a grown-up' but your children's exams are
even worse! Much! –

He stops suddenly and looks at STELLA. *He realises he
shouldn't be talking about children. He changes the subject
rapidly.*

GIDEON: Of all the places, in all the world – to come here,
Stella, to *relax* . . . ! That is wonderfully perverse!

STELLA: Oh, this won't relax you. (*She smiles cheerfully.*)
I promise you this won't be relaxing in the slightest
degree . . . (*She grins.*) That's got you interested now,
hasn't it!

*They stop. They are staring across the waste ground
towards a modern church, a triangular-shaped building
standing incongruously in the middle of this vast
wasteland.*

GIDEON: Oh, that's it?

STELLA: That's the one.

INT. MODERN CHURCH. DAY

*We cut inside the stark modern interior of the church. There is
a large choir of forty people standing waiting to perform. Some
are wearing bright-blue robes and some bright-red. The effect is
loud and brash. The choir is spread across the whole church,
in different groupings.*

STELLA *and* GIDEON *are sitting in the pews, watching. There
is absolutely nobody else in the audience. Round the edge of the*

church various women are cleaning, with their backs turned
towards the choristers. STELLA *waves to her friend, Sal, a large*
black woman in the choir.

  GIDEON *is staring at the choristers – large overweight boys,*
tiny small women, very thin bird-like men, plump round men,
some extremely large women. The whole choir seems full of
oddly-shaped people, vivid faces.

  The CHOIRMASTER *appears, a rather bombastic man with*
heavy glasses.

CHOIRMASTER: So – we're ready? We've got an audience
    for this rehearsal. (*Staring at* GIDEON *and* STELLA.)
    For which we are grateful. (*Rather fiercely.*) Anybody
    not ready? So – there's nothing to stop us!

  The choir start singing Tallis's evocative anthem 'Spem in
alium' – insistent and surprisingly sensual music.

  Out of these oddly-shaped faces comes a magnificent
burst of sound. The sheer weight of it takes GIDEON
completely by surprise. It bounces off the walls of the empty
church. The cleaning ladies are still cleaning, but the music
totally envelopes him.

  GIDEON *looks across at* STELLA: *she is sitting ramrod*
straight in her pew. The music is getting louder and louder.
GIDEON *can see* STELLA *shaking very slightly as she sits*
bolt upright. We move in on STELLA.

  There is a cut to her son, the twelve-year-old boy,
moving out of the door of their house, wheeling his bicycle.
He is waving goodbye. The door begins to close and he
disappears out of shot, then his face suddenly comes round
the door with a grin one last time, and then he is gone.

  We cut back to STELLA. *We then see her big burly*
husband, BILL, *dragging the woman* PETERSEN, *the*
council leader, down the street. Then we see BILL *attacking*
the cycle lanes with a pickaxe, then we see him vaulting
over the road hump in the middle of the street swinging his

pickaxe, and then we see quick cuts of BILL *attacking other pieces of street furniture: extended pavements, raised ridges, extra bollards.*

We cut back to STELLA. *She is shaking, determined not to cry. She stares at the oddly-shaped faces making the glorious music. The anthem is building and building all the time.*

Suddenly STELLA *gets up.*

EXT. OUTSIDE CHURCH. INDUSTRIAL LANDSCAPE. DAY
We cut outside. We are in front of the church with the industrial landscape surrounding it on all sides. The music is continuing to leak out of the front door of the church. STELLA *is walking sharply away from the church, smoking.* GIDEON *catches her up.*

STELLA: I'm sorry . . . I didn't think I'd have to leave.
I don't usually have to leave. Bit bloody pointless, getting you all the way here . . . and then getting upset and running out!

GIDEON (*softly*): It's all right . . . I could see you were getting upset.

STELLA (*trying to joke*): And I could see you thinking – blimey, it's like the bloody restaurant she took me to, it's really quite good!

GIDEON (*grins*): That's exactly what I was thinking –
STELLA *is turning away from him as she feels the tears coming back.*

STELLA: I always get, you know, a bit 'moved' when I come, naturally . . . But I don't have to leave, not usually!

GIDEON: Is it because I am here?

STELLA: No, no. (*She's moving all the time.*) You know grief is . . . well – (*She turns, trying to smile.*) is hell, obviously – But we've got to this moment now . . .
I've got to this moment . . . when people are saying, or at least you can see it in their eyes, 'Surely it's time

to move on, just a little bit?' . . . 'Surely it's getting
less?' Well no, actually, it's not getting less! I'm sorry,
but it's not the slightest bit less.

GIDEON (*softly, near her*): Of course it isn't –

STELLA (*suddenly defiantly*): Bill is right not to let go! . . .
I was just thinking in there – however crazy it seems –
he's absolutely right not to let go . . . Everything is
over so quick now, on to the next thing, get rid of it –
think positively! . . . And I do try – I do really try . . .

GIDEON (*smiles*): I've noticed –

STELLA: But I come here . . . I have no faith, I don't
believe, not at all – never did. But I come here . . . to
this out-of-the-way church – because I need to feel
how much . . . (*She begins to cry.*) I need to feel if only
I had gone with him that first time . . . I need to think
that over and over, again and again . . . I need to ask,
WHY THE HELL DIDN'T I DO THAT? . . . GO
WITH HIM?! (*A real shout.*) WHY?! I need to do that
over and over . . . . That's why I come here . . .
   STELLA *is really crying.*

GIDEON: Stella . . . (*Gently.*) Let me . . . (*He takes her in
his arms.*)

STELLA: No, I don't want to be held. Not now. (*She breaks
away.*) Because I don't want you to think this is likely
to happen again . . .

GIDEON (*softly*): It's got to happen again, hasn't it – why
shouldn't it happen again?

STELLA: Because – don't get angry about this . . . You like
being with me – because of the unexpected bits . . .
because you don't know what's going to happen, isn't
that right? But you don't want to be reminded by
the other stuff, have that always hanging in the air,
coming up all the time, because you'll feel you can't
talk about your daughter . . . because she's with you,
she's alive . . .

GIDEON: Of course I won't feel that . . . That's not true
at all.

STELLA: We'll see. (*She moves close to him, touches him.*)
We'll see if I am right . . . (*She kisses him.*) I don't
want to be right . . . !

INT. GIDEON'S FLAT. DAY

We cut to NATASHA *sitting in the window-seat in her room,
calmly waiting. We see her in long-shot along the length of the
apartment. She is sitting very poised, facing us.*

GIDEON *and* STELLA *are moving towards her, the camera
subjectively tracking towards her.* STELLA *is hanging back, a
few paces behind* GIDEON.

GIDEON: Hi darling . . . (*He turns.*) this is a friend of
mine . . . Stella Hawthorne.

STELLA *smiles at her.*

NATASHA: Hi . . .

STELLA: Hello . . .

There is a pause. NATASHA *does not move from the
window-seat.*

GIDEON: Has the deadline passed?

NATASHA: Yes . . . I still want to go.

GIDEON*'s eyes flicker.*

NATASHA: But I know if I go I will never hear the end of it
and of course you won't give me any money . . . So,
at the moment, I'm thinking I can't go to South
America . . . If I go to Edinburgh I will not be staying
in halls of residence. It's going to be somewhere else.
Her dark eyes stare straight at GIDEON. GIDEON *nods,
trying to conceal how massively relieved he is.*

INT. THE CABINET OFFICE PASSAGES. EVENING

The camera is moving fast down a passage towards the Cabinet Office as an official hurries to get to the meeting.

SNEATH (*voice-over*): And so the great meeting . . . He is on a high . . . he is elated . . .

We enter the room, a very grand nineteenth-century office hung with portraits. It is full of civil servants and politicians. DENT *is sitting at a very large desk with two extremely senior civil servants next to him, and also an empty chair as if they are waiting for somebody to join them.*

Opposite them GIDEON *is sitting in a very relaxed way, his legs stretched out.* ANDREW *is sitting just behind him, just by his shoulder. As we enter the room* DENT *is in mid-sentence.*

DENT: – and Peter will be joining us in a moment . . . and it's possible the Prime Minister as well . . .

SNEATH (*voice-over*): And Gideon is *so* high, he just talks, making it up on the spur of the moment, whatever comes into his head.

GIDEON: I think I know what we should do in the Dome. Paradise . . . a jungle, a thick jungle. Like the French painter Rousseau . . .

The room tenses at the mention of a foreign painter.

No, don't worry about the French bit . . . a great natural environment showing the glories of the planet, with electric beasts lurking in the rainforest, in real tropical environments . . . We show the whole lot, the desert, the Arctic . . . intense tropical colour! And then the future, whatever technology we celebrate comes out of the glories of our natural world . . . There will be rides, little trains running through a landscape so vivid you will be able to touch it, to drink it and the smell of flowers will be completely intoxicating.

SNEATH (*voice-over*): All he's talking about is a gigantic
greenhouse! But they are entranced – and of course
he was onto a potential hit . . . and as he's talking . . .
whether it is his imagination or not, the room is
getting fuller and fuller –
We see the room really full of officials in dark suits.
– until it's like some grand nineteenth-century
painting, with them all looking at Gideon!

GIDEON (*staring at all the officials watching him intently*):
And outside London what we do is this – we celebrate
the creativity of the community with incredible
singing . . . arias from stages floating down the main
rivers of the country . . . churches on industrial estates
lit up by searchlights and their concerts magnified on
the biggest screens anybody has ever seen . . .
We see the room still filling with people, come to listen to
GIDEON.

INT. ITALIAN RESTAURANT. DAY
We cut to SNEATH, *sitting eating opposite* GIDEON *at a table in
the window of a small, fashionable Italian restaurant.* GIDEON
is looking very elegant and is laughing and joking with SNEATH.

SNEATH (*voice-over*): And so here we have a man who
can't listen – and yet the more he doesn't listen the
more people want him, the more people believe in him.
He is the toast of Whitehall, the flavour of all flavours.

GIDEON: Extraordinary thing is they have no idea what to
put in it. This bloody Dome . . .
SNEATH *chuckling.*

GIDEON: In the Lake District, there is a pencil museum in
Cumbria. There is! And I said – they will, they will do
better business inside your Dome than you will if you
fill it with zones and lists . . . I told them!
He is laughing.

SNEATH (*voice-over*): And I wanted to be with him too.
I loved seeing him. I always did. I had no inkling
anything was amiss.
There is a loud knocking on the sound track.

INT. SNEATH'S APARTMENT AND PASSAGE. DAY
The knocking is sharp and loud. SNEATH's *face turns sharply.*
He is wearing his pyjama top by now. We cut outside into the
passage of the mansion flats. A tiny boy of about four is standing
knocking at the door and ringing the doorbell. SNEATH *opens*
the door and sees the tiny boy.
SNEATH: Frederick! My little one! All alone . . . ?
He sees a woman's shadow disappearing right at the far
end of the passage.
Your mum . . . just a disappearing shadow now . . .
That is what it has come to has it?! . . . The nearest
she'll come . . . ! (*He stares sadly down the passage for*
a fraction of a second, then he turns back to the little boy.)
I hadn't forgotten my little one . . . I promise you! . . .
Just ignore the pyjamas . . .
Time cut. We cut inside the flat. Frederick is sitting on the
floor, BECCA *is looking at him entranced.* SNEATH *is busy*
opening cupboards and drawers.
SNEATH: Somewhere . . . I have some toys hidden – some
good ones too!
He finds some toys triumphantly. BECCA *meanwhile is*
touching the boy's head.
BECCA: Hello, darling . . . What a lovely boy.
SNEATH: Come here, let's take this off. Come on, it's all
right, take it off – all right all right, leave it on.
The little boy has clenched up, not allowing his father to
take his coat off.
SNEATH: He was alone in the passage . . . Christ Almighty,
just standing there! . . . (*He lifts the little boy onto his*

knee.) You never stop worrying about them . . . I have
three, would you believe – the other two are much
older . . . (*He holds the little boy.*) Beat, beat, beat, it's
always there somewhere in your brain, the worry
about them . . .

EXT./INT. GIDEON'S APARTMENT. DAY
We see GIDEON *staring down through the window of his
apartment, watching* NATASHA *disappearing down the street.*
SNEATH (*voice-over*): And this is what was happening to
Gideon. She didn't talk to him . . . he could never
find her most of the time . . . she stayed out for many
nights, she didn't ring. Her love had gone. A worm
enters his head, a worm in his thoughts telling him he
had made a great mistake forcing her to stay . . . and
that somehow something bad would happen . . . that
she would engineer it or just simple old fate would do
it for her . . .

INT. GIDEON'S APARTMENT. LATE AFTERNOON
We cut to NATASHA *in a fifties ball-gown, moving backwards
and forwards in her room. The door is open and we can see her
through the whole expanse of the apartment. She looks magical
in her dress as she moves. It is late afternoon and the sun is a
rich colour.* NATASHA *seems to glow in her period dress as she
gets herself ready.*

GIDEON *is watching her from a distance.*

BARBARA *is sitting with him, but leaning forward in a tense
way, trying to engage* GIDEON's *attention.*
BARBARA: She looks gorgeous, doesn't she . . . ? (*Then she
calls out:*) Natasha, you look terrific!
NATASHA: I hate fancy-dress parties – and 'come dressed
as a fifties character' is really difficult –

BARBARA: And who are you dressed as?

NATASHA: I don't know . . . a fifties movie star – not Marilyn Monroe . . . somebody English . . . were there any fifties British movie stars . . . ?

GIDEON: I think she is dressed as my mother . . . She was very beautiful, my mum . . . one of my first memories of her was in a dress like that . . .

GIDEON watches his daughter. BARBARA leans towards GIDEON.

BARBARA: Every time I go out at the moment, every meeting, people talk about you, do you realise that? . . . 'I heard Gideon is thinking this' . . . 'I want to talk to Gideon about that' . . . 'I hear Gideon Warner may be interested' . . . The number of people I have heard say – 'I'm hoping to have lunch with Gideon Warner soon . . . '!

She's watching GIDEON, his face is half-turned away.

BARBARA: But I look at you –

She pauses; GIDEON doesn't look at her.

BARBARA: I look at you – and you're somewhere completely different. Certainly for me. I know you think I never notice anything – (*Sad smile.*) that I miss everything that's interesting – but I have noticed *that.*

She looks at him; he is still watching NATASHA getting ready.

BARBARA: Maybe we should have a pause . . .

He doesn't react.

You know, a pause in seeing each other Gideon . . . ?

GIDEON (*quiet*): If you think so . . .

BARBARA: 'If I think so . . . '! That's all?

GIDEON turns and looks directly at her.

GIDEON: She goes to university on Saturday. It's a big moment. For so many years she's been just down the corridor from me. (*He calls out.*) Natasha, I've got something here for you. I know you've always said

you'd be the last person in England to have one – but
I've bought you a mobile phone.

NATASHA *stands in the doorway of her room in her ball-*
gown.

NATASHA: You've bought me a phone? (*Sharply.*) It really
goes with my costume, Dad . . . !

Time cut. It is dusk now. GIDEON *is sitting in the near*
darkness. The television is on: he is playing the tape of
NATASHA *singing her song 'Papa', her one eye looking at*
him. He is staring at it with such concentration he doesn't
notice BARBARA *leave the apartment. She watches him*
a moment from the doorway and then slips away.

We cut back to the tape and GIDEON *watching.*

NATASHA *approaches out of the shadows. She is fully*
made up now and wearing pearls, her hair is done in a
fifties style. She looks like Grace Kelly. She comes right
up to him.

GIDEON: You look wonderful. (*He looks at her standing in*
the twilight.) Absolutely sensational! . . .

NATASHA (*simply*): Good.

GIDEON: I should find a movie première to go to . . . The
celebrities would be clamouring to meet you –

NATASHA: I don't want to go to any of those ever again . . .

GIDEON *turns in surprise.* NATASHA *is watching herself*
on the screen for a moment.

NATASHA: Why are you looking at that song?

GIDEON: Because I can't get it out of my head . . .

NATASHA *is standing in her ball-gown staring down at*
him.

NATASHA: I told you . . . it was just a song, Dad.

She is standing half-silhouetted in the falling light.

GIDEON: I love you so much.

NATASHA *just stares back impassively.*

SNEATH (*voice-over*): She looked so beautiful . . . It was
like a last picture of her.

We see NATASHA *moving through the door, half-turning to look back at* GIDEON.

We move in on GIDEON, *a very intense close-up.*

INT. SNEATH'S APARTMENT. DAY

We cut to SNEATH, *who is now dressed in shirt and trousers. He is about to put on his shoes and socks.*

SNEATH: When they go to university it's like a death, a little death, but we're never allowed to talk about it like that . . .

INT. STELLA'S SITTING ROOM. AFTERNOON

We cut to STELLA *and* GIDEON *lying under the fine bed cover after having made love. They are both staring up at the clouds on the ceiling.*

STELLA: You know they light up? . . . I haven't shown you this?! This is worth seeing!

She flicks a switch just behind her: the clouds light up, little wall-lights pointing upwards.

There! (*She laughs.*) Not bad, eh . . . ?

GIDEON: Very impressive. An instant heaven!

STELLA: Very few people get to see that . . . in fact no one, I don't think . . . !

GIDEON: I'm honoured. (*He smiles.*) Absolutely. Talking of which – I had a call from the Prime Minister yesterday. The Number Ten switchboard calls (*He mimics a strict middle-aged woman's voice.*) 'I'm putting you through now . . . ' Then absolutely nothing happens . . . then this voice: 'The Prime Minister will talk to you in ten minutes' . . . Then again, 'I'm putting you through now' . . . And then there he is: 'I hear you are doing even more wonderful things for the Millennium . . . you must come and talk to me personally.'

STELLA: Great! I bet that receptionist gets to hear a few
things . . . (*Imitating.*) 'I'm putting you through now.'
I'd love to *be* her, ringing up cabinet ministers when
they are going to be sacked, a voice of doom. (*She
imitates.*) 'The Prime Minister would like to see you
in exactly one hour's time', it'll be great, the death
sentence . . . ! And she's able to find anybody
wherever they are in the world – that receptionist . . .

She sees GIDEON *is half-turned away from her.*

STELLA: Even your daughter . . .

GIDEON *turns back.*

STELLA: You *can* talk about her you know – about
wondering what she's up to . . . about when you'll hear
from her . . . (*With feeling.*) *Talk* to me about that . . .

GIDEON (*closed off from her*): It's fine. There is nothing to
say about her.

We stay on STELLA*'s eyes.*

INT. CONFERENCE ROOM FOR FOCUS GROUP. DAY
We cut to ANDREW *and some officials looking through a
mirrored wall at a focus group sitting round a large table. They
are being shown pictures of the Millennium Dome and then
various cards about what should go inside: cards that show
various futuristic machines, animals, theme-park rides, showbiz
symbols. We see* GIDEON *is standing with* STELLA *further down
the mirrored wall and they are laughing and joking together.*
ANDREW *stares at* STELLA *with suspicion.* GIDEON *is dialling
his daughter on his mobile phone.*

STELLA: Leave her . . . don't try to reach her . . . it's fine!

She confiscates his mobile, GIDEON *lets her do this.*

STELLA *stares at the focus group sitting round the table.*

STELLA: What an amazingly boring bunch . . . I told you
so, didn't I?

ANDREW *is simultaneously talking to the officials around him as they stare at the group.*

ANDREW: In the old days we used to guess what people wanted – which meant we told them what we thought was good for them . . . It amazes me how recently we still did that! Now we really know what they want and we better listen . . .

We see GIDEON *moving close to the wall. As he stares at the people round the table they begin to transform. He sees a different collection sitting there, hairy men with tattoos, a crazy-looking woman with pigtails, a tiny little professor with a huge long white beard, an extremely tall man dressed entirely in black wearing a hat.* GIDEON *laughs, as does* STELLA *realising what he is doing.*

The camera tracks in on ANDREW *as he watches the two of them closely.*

INT. THE SPORTS CAFÉ. NIGHT

We are inside a sports café – many flickering screens, indoor tennis playing on some, American football on others. The place is full of shadows and different colours and hard edges. There are a few people drinking and eating in the shadows. ANDREW, STELLA *and* GIDEON *are sitting at a table drinking cocktails.* ANDREW *is also eating quite a hearty meal. As he eats, he glances at all the screens.*

ANDREW: My favourite place of the moment . . .

One of the televisions is showing the news. There is an item about the murder of two young women, taking place just hours apart, in Edinburgh. GIDEON *is watching the item over his shoulder, tensely.* STELLA *follows his look.* ANDREW *is waving a fork in the direction of the television.*

ANDREW: Nowhere is safe any more, is it . . . ? When we are finished with the Millennium, we'll have to start rebranding our streets . . .

GIDEON *is still staring at the television. One of the*
waitresses flicks channels. It goes over to more sports.
GIDEON *is still staring at the screen for a moment, then*
turns back.

ANDREW: You OK?

ANDREW *is staring at him very directly.* GIDEON *doesn't*
immediately answer. He takes a sip of his drink and stares
right back at ANDREW.

GIDEON: Andrew can't work out if I've lost the plot or not –

STELLA: Does that matter in your business – how would
anybody tell the difference?!

GIDEON (*still meeting* ANDREW*'s stare*): You're thinking
that – despite all the work we're currently getting –
you're wondering has he lost it?

ANDREW: Well, I think either you've gone into a
stratosphere so high-powered, I can't follow you
there . . . Or –

GIDEON: Or . . . ?

ANDREW: Or something else is going on . . .

GIDEON: Such as what?

ANDREW: Ah! (*He is eating voraciously.*) I'm working that
out.

GIDEON: And when you've worked it out, what will you
do about it?

ANDREW: If, and there are a lot of 'if's here . . . if I
discovered I was working for somebody who was
indulging in a son-of-an-immigrant guilt trip – 'Is this
what my father hoped I'd do?' – or 'I'm really too
good for this shallow work' trip – (*He eats another*
mouthful.) Or if I was working for somebody who
started being uneasy about exercising power, it's
all a bit too mundane and political – so let's tiptoe
away . . . (*He munches food.*) Then that would call
for action –

GIDEON: And what would that action be?

ANDREW (*smiles as he chews*): And there's another if . . .
if I thought I was working for somebody who had
deliberately hired a bright young guy full of energy
who reminded him a little bit of his younger self, and
he thought let's play with this young guy for a while,
give him his head – and then, whoops, he's getting a
bit scary now, a bit too focused . . . so let's distance
ourselves from all that fast . . . !

GIDEON: If that was the case, you'd be off, you'd be gone
as quick as you could to a competitor –

ANDREW: You think . . . ? (*He takes another mouthful.*) If
I was working for somebody like that – I wouldn't
leave. I would stay right in his face working out why
he was trying so hard to throw it all away . . . I would
be there when he woke up in the morning, I'd be
there at night when his head hit the pillow . . . and I'd
be at the end of the bed when he finished shagging . . .
That's what I would do. (*He smiles straight at* GIDEON.)
Dingle, dingle, dingle . . . there I would be . . . !
STELLA *has been drinking her cocktail through a straw,
she takes the straw out of her mouth.*

STELLA: Not when I'm around, you won't!
ANDREW *is staring at* GIDEON. GIDEON *smiles.*

GIDEON: Good food, is that?

ANDREW: It's great.
GIDEON *helps himself to a tiny taste off* ANDREW's *plate.
He eats it and then looks at* ANDREW *with a dangerous
smile.*

GIDEON: I think it's time to show you the best food in
London, Andrew . . . and a lot of other people, too.

EXT. STAR OF THE ORIENT. NIGHT
We cut outside the Star of the Orient. There is a red carpet,
there is one searchlight stabbing the sky. There are various large
cars rolling up and depositing a selection of stars and VIPs.
SNEATH (*voice-over*): So we all find ourselves being invited
    to this eatery in Southall. It was a time when parties
    were being held in the oddest venues – in meat
    markets, in deserted underground stations – so
    nobody at first thought it was particularly strange . . .
We see many of the faces we saw at the movie première
at the beginning when the red carpet was awash with
detergent. This time the red carpet is decorated with flowers
but there is only a small curious crowd of local inhabitants
watching the stars arrive.

    The onlookers include some buskers, a tramp, three
plump schoolgirls, and a dog sitting on the edge of the
carpet on its own.

    We see BADALAMENTI *entering with his bodyguards,*
giving the meagre crowd a dazzling smile and ruffling the
head of the dog who looks at him suspiciously.

    We see the starlet DIANE *arrive in a beautiful white*
dress. We see DENT *with his entourage.*

INT. STAR OF THE ORIENT. NIGHT
We cut inside the interior with its red elephant heads and
white-and-gold décor. Tonight there are some additional
decorations, more garlands, and huge paper flowers staring
down. We move with SNEATH *as he weaves his way along the*
red carpet and inside the restaurant. He catches glimpses of
the small AMERICAN PRODUCER *with the enormous glasses;*
he passes ANDREW, *who is on the prowl, gossiping, eyeing the*
surprising mixture of guests.

    STELLA *is standing in the middle of the restaurant, like*
a joint host; she is wearing a splendid dress and introducing

people to each other. We see in among the celebrities and film
executives and politicians, are Hanif from the twenty-four-hour
store and the boy in leather who haunts the store, and members
of the church choir from Wolverhampton. We also glimpse, in the
corner, her husband, BILL, *who is wearing a very smart suit.*

STELLA: Hello, I'm Stella. I'm co-hosting the evening.
This is Mr Singh, he owns the restaurant, Hanif my
boss . . .
We see the politician DENT, *sitting with a fashionable*
young woman.

DENT: Is there anybody here who might be able to tell us
what the bloody hell we're doing here?
GIDEON *is moving through the throng, looking elegant*
and smiling at all the guests. But as we cut close, we stay
on his eyes, we see the gathering from his viewpoint, faces
are blurred, the sound strange. To the outside world he looks
just the same, effortlessly in charge, but when we get inside
his head we see how much he is floating, how detached he
has become. The AMERICAN PRODUCER *comes up to him.*

AMERICAN PRODUCER: What's so special about this place?
Should I have heard of it?

GIDEON (*glancing across the room*): My daughter may make
it tonight . . . I'm hoping . . .
He takes out his phone and checks it. SNEATH *sees*
GIDEON *through the crowd, but he cannot reach him.*
We cut to BILL *in the corner talking to* GIDEON.

BILL: I really am looking forward to tonight, you know.
We cut to STELLA, *who has already had several drinks,*
coming up to BADALAMENTI.

STELLA: Mr Badalamenti, you won't know me, but I'm a
friend of Gideon's, how do you do!

BADALAMENTI: Charming of course to meet a friend of
Gideon's –

STELLA: So what are you going to buy over here? Some
of our newspapers, or all our TV stations? (*Smiles.*)

Going to give us housewives stripping? And naked
newsreaders?

BADALAMENTI (*in mellow mood*): I hope so, why not?
Maybe even politicians stripping, who knows! If
they're given their own TV show they will pass all the
right legislation! (*Then, searching the crowd.*) So where
is Mr Gideon? He hasn't said hello to me . . . which
is too strange . . .

We see ANDREW *prowling amongst the guests.*

SNEATH *is glancing across and sees* STELLA *and*
BADALAMENTI *together.*

SNEATH (*voice-over*): I see this confident-looking woman,
talking to all these important people, I'm beginning
to feel jealous – who is she? Is she writing a book too
about Gideon?!

SNEATH *pushes his way through the crush; he sees* STELLA
introduce herself to DIANE, *the starlet, who is standing just
by an enormous ornamental elephant head.*

DIANE (*to* STELLA): I just need to find Gideon . . . he gave
me some advice . . . (*Her beautiful face anxious.*) Just
want to check it with him one more time –

SNEATH *is forcing his way through the guests trying to
find* GIDEON. *He sees the celebrities eyeing the local people
who have also been invited – the celebrities trying to work
out who on earth these normal people are. The owner of
the restaurant is beaming at the VIPs and they nod
awkwardly back.*

We cut to STELLA *and* BILL, *moving through the crowd
to confront* DENT, *who is sitting in a corner surrounded by
some young media types and his own assistants.*

STELLA: Hello, Mr Dent . . .

DENT *tenses when he sees* BILL.

BILL: Don't worry, your hair is safe . . . (*Slight laugh.*) For
tonight at least . . . !

DENT (*choosing his words with great care*): Well, that is something I'm most reassured to hear. We all turned up for the demonstration didn't we . . . ?

BILL: You did. And what did you think? What did you conclude when it happened?

STELLA *is watching* DENT *closely.*

DENT: I concluded . . . I saw somebody who was in pain. In grief.

BILL: Yes . . . that is certainly true. And what did you think I accomplished?

DENT: Well, you let a lot of rage come out at elected officials – officials that are too busy or too over-stretched to use their common sense . . .

STELLA: That is a surprise. An admission! Why didn't you ever say anything like that to us before . . . ?

DENT: You think a Member of Parliament can go round admitting he's hated by the local council . . . and that's why they won't co-operate . . . ? It doesn't mean I don't understand how important it was to get us together – (*Suddenly.*) Not all politicians are shits, you know . . . (*Sharp smile.*) I'm really sick and tired of seeing all politicians dismissed as two-faced careerists who won't listen. We work so bloody hard! You'd be surprised!

BILL*'s huge face close to* DENT.

BILL: You work hard, I'm sure. You want me to think better of you? . . . Then I will – when you start to think all members of the public who won't let go of something, who go on and on, are not *damaged* people . . . (*He sits opposite* DENT, *almost squashing him.*) I am *reduced* by my son's death . . . of course . . . I am reduced compared to what I was . . . I am slower, I'm clumsier, I don't tell many jokes now – but I am not out of my mind . . . ! (*He sips the drink.*)

Quite the opposite . . . And I got the cycle lane rerouted. *I* did that!

We are moving with SNEATH *backstage, past all the waiters laden with food and through into the kitchen.*

SNEATH (*voice-over*): And then I find him . . . he is there among the spices and all the different dishes laid out – GIDEON *is standing right in the corner of the kitchen.*

SNEATH (*voice-over*): And amongst all that food, squashed into a corner, as if retreating from everything.

SNEATH: Gideon.

GIDEON: Yes?

SNEATH: What are you doing here?

GIDEON: Just staying out of trouble.

SNEATH (*voice-over*): He tells me about his daughter, and the song and the French mystery writer with all his lovers, about Stella, about how sort of removed he feels from everything . . . how he can't get his daughter on the phone, hasn't heard from her for weeks . . . He looks so like the normal Gideon . . . but all the time he is talking to me he is looking over my shoulder –

We see a TV across the kitchen, with news about the murdered girls in Edinburgh and how the police are still appealing for witnesses.

We cut to ANDREW *moving among the throng – looking bewildered and slightly lost, unable to understand what the occasion is for, unable to find* GIDEON.

ANDREW (*as he moves among the people, muttering to himself*): I don't know why a lot of these people are here . . . I don't know who they are . . . (*He turns to someone.*) Have you seen Gideon? . . . Where is Gideon? *We cut back to the kitchens.* GIDEON's *face close to* SNEATH.

GIDEON: I just need a breath of fresh air . . .

We cut to SNEATH *re-entering the main room and surveying all the people.*

SNEATH (*voice-over*): He was gone before I could say
    anything . . . and there is a strange sensation in that
    restaurant . . . all these people looking for Gideon, it's
    like a shadow has descended . . . Like at the end of
    this very odd summer – when there has been all this
    hysteria about the death of a princess, and all the
    flowers – where was the man, the man they needed,
    who helped so many of them understand what they
    should do next . . . ? And as I'm standing there . . .
    I see people I haven't noticed before in the crowd . . .
    people from Gideon's past . . . like the old comedians
    Crumb and Yardley, Miller and Dave . . .
    We see the plump old comedians chain-smoking and
    laughing loudly. SNEATH *pushes his way through the*
    guests: the scene has become hallucinatory as the celebrities
    move in bewildered circles under the staring elephants and
    the loud wallpaper.

    SNEATH *sees* STELLA *and is drawn towards her. She is*
    looking worried.

SNEATH: Are you Stella?

STELLA: Yes . . . I know who you are . . . Have you seen
    Gideon?

SNEATH (*casually*): He's just popped out for a breath of
    fresh air . . .
    They both stand and survey the guests as they mill all
    around them, the celebrities faces full of confusion.
    You know, it's like he has got all these people
    together, in this weird place, to say 'Grow up . . . you
    don't need me, to hell with celebrity . . . !'

STELLA (*quietly*): I know where he has gone . . . He has
    gone to find her . . .

EXT. EDINBURGH. DAY

We see GIDEON *staring down over Edinburgh from one of the vantage points of the city. His back is to us. The camera is moving slowly towards him. He is still dressed in his dinner jacket from the party.*

SNEATH (*voice-over*): Here's a man willing his daughter to
　　be safe . . . It's as if by thinking about her strongly
　　enough, and staring across the city, he can keep her
　　out of harm's way.

INT. EDINBURGH. STUDENT HOSTEL. DAY

We see GIDEON *running up the stone steps of an old block of student flats. He's ringing the doorbell; his manner is contained, not frantic. A young girl opens the door. The scene is viewed in a long shot from across the landing.*

GIDEON: Have you seen Natasha?

　　The girl shakes her head.

　　When was she last here?

INT. LONDON MANSION FLAT. DAY

We cut from the stone steps of the Edinburgh hostel to the plush passage of the London mansion flats. SNEATH, BECCA *and* Frederick *are setting off for a walk.*

SNEATH: And I'm thinking Becca as I keep trying to get
　　Gideon after the party . . . I'm thinking about signs . . .
　　I'm thinking those wretched murders in Scotland are
　　not relevant, are not the point . . . I'm thinking much
　　more about that song, in *particular* that song,
　　Natasha's song . . . !

　　We hear it on the soundtrack, the lilting tune and NATASHA's
　　*voice singing it. We see the flowers, the petals descending on
　　the day* GIDEON *saw* BILL *at the park, and then we see the
　　flowers on the red carpet outside the Star of the Orient.*

SNEATH (*voice-over*): And I'm going through the images . . .
in my mind – of that summer.

EXT. EDINBURGH STREET. DAY

We see GIDEON *moving along the Edinburgh streets, looking at
the faces of the young people as they brush past him.*

SNEATH (*voice-over*): And I'm thinking a song about
obsessive love . . . and somebody that takes their own
life . . . It's the girl who did that, who killed herself –
but flip Natasha's song, turn it round . . . and it's
about her *dad*, it's about Gideon – *his* love is too
strong . . . And then the thought enters my head –
he has not just gone to Edinburgh in case harm has
befallen her . . . but rather to say goodbye . . .

We see GIDEON *moving away from us down the street –
his progress not desperate, he is very detached from
everything he sees. We see him enter a dingy little club.*

SNEATH (*voice-over*): There's *one* thing that links father
and daughter – he has looked after all those comics,
and Natasha has a great love for stand-up . . .

We see GIDEON *sitting in the shadows of a tiny club,
studying the audience as an unseen comedian cracks jokes.
The camera moves in on* GIDEON'*s face in the dark.*

EXT. LONDON PARK. DAY

We see SNEATH, *the tiny Frederick and* BECCA *walking in a
London park.* BECCA'*s face looks anxious and sad, as they
walk in silence for a moment.*

INT. EDINBURGH COMEDY CLUB. EVENING

*We cut to an audience exploding into loud laughter as a stand-
up comic is in full flight.* GIDEON *suddenly appears at the back*

*of this larger comedy club. The comic breaks off his monologue
in the middle of a sentence when* GIDEON *enters rather loudly
at the back.*

COMIC: Better late than never! Our friend is looking for
a seat . . . for the last seven minutes of the show . . .
obviously he has heard they're the best bit. AND
HE'S NOT WRONG! Normally I kill latecomers . . .
I use the meat-hooks up there . . . but somebody give
him a seat . . .

GIDEON *is staring around the theatre. He sees* NATASHA
near the front. She turns and looks at him as GIDEON
moves towards her down the aisle, in full view of everybody.
NATASHA *looks very startled but not hostile.*

*People are laughing uneasily, embarrassed, shifting in
their seats.*

COMIC: Determined fellow isn't he . . . ?!

The COMIC *continues to take advantage of the situation,
pouring jokes out, throwing them at* GIDEON, *humiliating
him in front of the audience.*

GIDEON *continues down the aisle, crosses onto the stage
and stands next to the* COMIC. *He turns for a fleeting
moment looking at* NATASHA *and then goes through the
door at the back of the auditorium.*

NATASHA *stares after him. The* COMIC *admonishes the
audience.*

COMIC: This is all your fault, you bad people . . . !
Something very wrong with you all, obviously. He
takes one look at you – and he is off! He is out of
here!

The sound begins to blur. As NATASHA *is moving out of
her seat, as the audience is laughing all around her, the*
COMIC *is continuing his act.*

We see NATASHA *moving after* GIDEON. *He is in a
narrow passage, sitting in a corner on the floor. He is not*

curled up, but he is sitting awkwardly, strangely, as if he
is unable to move.

We track with NATASHA *as she approaches him. She*
sinks to her knees, she bends over him. We see her touch
him, but in a light detached way. She is running her
hands up his sleeve, then takes his hand. She sees he is
breathing fine – he is looking at her, but he still seems
unable, or reluctant, to move.

The camera is some distance away staring at them
down the passage; as she touches him, we can't quite hear.
She is leaning near him, lightly touching his hair.

We cut close. GIDEON *is watching her, he says nothing.*

NATASHA: My phone was broken . . . I should have let you
know . . . (*She runs her hand through his hair.*) I'm here
now . . .

GIDEON *doesn't move. He can't move.*

NATASHA *turns his face towards her, quite forcefully.*
She holds his face in her hands. Her tone is direct, not
over-emotional.

NATASHA: I didn't want you in my thoughts . . . anywhere
near me, really . . . I didn't want to hear your voice . . .
or get your letters . . .
She whispers, their faces close.
But now . . . I think that's over . . . Wherever you are,
wherever I am . . . (*She touches his face.*) I won't let
that happen again . . .

EXT. LONDON PARK. DAY
We cut to BECCA *and* SNEATH *and Frederick in the park.*
BECCA *is holding the little boy's hand and staring intensely at*
SNEATH. SNEATH *sees her anxious to know.*
SNEATH: Not so cruel . . . she wasn't, was she? Was that
better, Becca . . . ? Something mysterious happened

in that passage; he couldn't move. Maybe she could talk to him . . . because he couldn't move . . . because he was defenceless. What did she hope to do with that song? Did she really want to tip him over the edge when she wrote it? We never know what's going on in our children's heads . . . (*He stares at little Frederick. He touches the boy's hair.*) Do they ever really forgive us . . . ?

INT. PASSAGE. COMEDY CLUB. EDINBURGH. EVENING
A huge roar of laughter from inside the theatre. We can hear the COMIC *getting to the climax of his monologue.* NATASHA *is bent over* GIDEON, *whispering.*

NATASHA: You have to admit – he is better than Crumb and Yardley . . . !
Wide shot of them alone in the passage.

NATASHA: Come on! Why can't you move, Dad? Come on.
She tries with all her strength to move him, to lift him. She wraps her arms round him and pulls and pulls. She cannot move him. She falls to her knees beside him, holding him.

INT. NATASHA'S STUDENT BEDROOM. MORNING
A close shot of GIDEON'S *eyes flashing open. For a moment he doesn't realise where he is. There is a tinkling sound. A wind-chime is dangling from the light above his head.*

STELLA *is sitting at the end of the bed.* NATASHA *is curled up asleep in the corner.*

STELLA: You wake, and it's not Andrew at the end of the bed, it's me . . .

GIDEON: Thank God for that . . . !

STELLA: How are you?

GIDEON: I don't think I know what happened . . . no idea
. . . everything just stopped . . . (*He smiles.*) I'm glad
to see you, that's for sure.

STELLA: And that's a start. You know what? I think we
should have a hefty slice of toast and marmalade . . .
particularly chunky marmalade . . . And *then* I think
it's time for us to venture a little further than
Wolverhampton or Sunderland. You and me . . .
Together . . .

GIDEON (*staring at her*): I think that's a great idea . . .

STELLA: Maybe we should start with a little walk, got to
get you moving again. You were frozen in that comedy
club . . . (*She grins.*) What a place to seize up!

NATASHA *is stirring. She turns and looks at them both.*

NATASHA: I'll come too . . . if you're going for a walk, I'll
come too.

EXT. EDINBURGH SQUARE. EARLY MORNING

GIDEON, STELLA *and* NATASHA *are walking across a square
in early morning light. Leaves are blowing across the pavement.
Church bells are ringing out. The empty street really echoing to
the sound of the bells.*

*We are moving with them as they walk for a moment in
silence.*

STELLA: Don't answer immediately . . . but I'm thinking
this is much more than a week – our trip . . .

GIDEON: The trip that is further than Wolverhampton . . . ?

STELLA: Yes. It's more than a month, I'm thinking . . .
Don't answer yet . . . ! What happens . . . ? What
happens, Gideon, if we go somewhere else in the
world and just see where it leads . . . ?! Get you away
from your work . . . Get me away from where my little
boy died . . . let Natasha go anywhere she wants –

because she will keep in touch . . . she will have a
satellite tag on her, won't she . . . ?!

NATASHA *smiles as they walk.*

GIDEON: Just see what happens? . . .

STELLA: Yes! (*Laughs.*) You let someone else sell the
Millennium! And I let someone else clear out the
guinea-pigs' shit? How about it? How about it,
Gideon?!

We watch them walk away from us. The bells are ringing.

SNEATH (*voice-over*): And then they vanish . . .

*We see the image of them dissolve as they vanish off the
street.*

*We stare at the empty street with the bells ringing
loudly.*

SNEATH (*voice-over*): One call for me from Gideon just
before they left – and then they vanish, and they've
stayed vanished all these years. Nobody knows what
happened to them . . . where they are roaming . . .
where they are now . . . Sometimes I think I see one
or other of them from a car or a taxi . . . I thought
I caught a glimpse of Natasha not so long ago . . . it
was her –

EXT. LONDON STREETS. DAY

We see a shot of NATASHA *moving confidently down a London
street, looking very sun-tanned and happy.*

SNEATH (*voice-over*): She was looking very radiant. Her
beauty was so strong, you felt Gideon would have
been able to feel it wherever he was in the world . . .
and however far she travelled . . . But then I don't
know that . . .

NATASHA *disappears from view amongst the people on the
pavement.*

EXT. LONDON PARK. DAY

We cut to SNEATH, BECCA *and little Frederick walking away from us in the park. We see the three of them disappearing down a long avenue of trees.*

SNEATH: And Stella and Gideon? . . . Have they found happiness? Who knows?! I tell you one thing, I bet they're still together . . . Is he driven mad worrying about Natasha in this dangerous world? . . . I don't know . . . The funny thing is – what a huge hole he left! On Millennium night . . . the plastic Dome . . . that ghastly beacon with the Queen . . . How did that happen?! The most important night for a thousand years, how on earth did we let that happen?!

> BECCA *and Frederick staring at* SNEATH *with their big eyes.*

SNEATH (*grins at them*): One thing though . . . ! In Wolverhampton . . . there was this church –

EXT. CHURCH IN INDUSTRIAL ESTATE. NIGHT

SNEATH (*voice-over*): And on Millennium night . . . ! When the clock struck twelve . . . !

> *We see a crane-shot moving towards the church, which is ablaze with light and colour. It has been lit up so it can be seen for miles around.*

I wish I could have been there . . . That was a sight to see!

> *The crane-shot reaches the church. The door is open. We see the vivid faces singing.*
>
> *The music of the oddly-shaped choir is pouring triumphantly out of the church's doors into the night air.*
>
> *Credits.*